P9-DGX-386

ESSENTIALS
for
LIFE
FOR WOMEN

Your Back to-Basics Guide to Simplifying Life
and Embracing What Matters Most

Marcia Ford

THOMAS NELSON
Since 1798

NASHVILLE   DALLAS   MEXICO CITY   RIO DE JANEIRO   BEIJING

Published in Nashville, Tennessee, by Thomas Nelson. Thomas Nelson is a trademark of Thomas Nelson, Inc.

Thomas Nelson, Inc., titles may be purchased in bulk for educational, business, fund-raising, or sales promotional use. For information, please e-mail Special Markets@ThomasNelson.com.

Scripture quotations marked CEV are from the *Contemporary English Version.* © 1991, 1992, 1995 by American Bible Society. Used by permission.

Scripture quotations marked ESV are taken from *The Holy Bible, English Standard Version,* © 2001 by Crossway Bibles, a division of Good News Publishers. Used by permission. All rights reserved.

Scripture quotations marked MSG are from *The Message* by Eugene H. Peterson, © 1993, 1994, 1995, 1996, 2000, 2001, 2002. Used by permission of NavPress Publishing Group. All rights reserved.

Scripture quotations marked NIV are taken from the *Holy Bible, New International Version.*® NIV®. © 1973, 1978, 1984, by International Bible Society. Used by permission of Zondervan. All rights reserved.

Scripture quotations noted NKJV are from THE NEW KING JAMES VERSION. © 1979, 1980, 1982, Thomas Nelson, Inc., Publishers.

Scripture quotations marked NLT are taken from *The Holy Bible, New Living Translation,* © 1996, 2004. Used by permission of Tyndale House Publishers, Inc., Wheaton, Illinois, 60189. All rights reserved.

Library of Congress Control Number: 2010920613

ISBN: 9780785229711

Editor: Lila Empson Wavering
Associate Editor: Jenn McNeil
Writer: Marcia Ford
Design: Whisner Design Group

Printed in the United States of America

10 11 12 13 14 WC 9 8 7 6 5 4 3 2 1

Streetwise people . . . are on constant alert, looking for angles, surviving by their wits. I want you to be smart in the same way—but for what is right—using every adversity to stimulate you to creative survival, to concentrate your attention on the bare essentials, so you'll live, really live, and not complacently just get by on good behavior.

Luke 16:8–9 MSG

ESSENTIALS *for* LIFE
FOR WOMEN
Contents

Nothing can separate you from
God's love, absolutely nothing. God
is enough for time, God is enough
for eternity. God is enough!

Hannah Whitall Smith

Introduction

Y ou can't do everything, but how do you know when you have done enough—or at least what was most important? Nearly every woman has heard this, felt this, said this. Deep down, you know it's true for you too. Listen to the TV or car radio for only a few minutes and you'll hear what a *responsible* woman should be concerned about, such as reducing her carbon footprint or lowering her overall cholesterol number.

It doesn't take long to start making a list of things you *should* do: volunteer at a homeless shelter, take a closer look at your retirement accounts, sort through things you don't use and have a yard sale, drive a more fuel-efficient car, plant the evergreen you've been promising yourself, do something nice for the neighbors. One thing always seems to lead to another.

Then there's that one-day-only sale you added to your calendar, the new, miracle antiwrinkle product you've wanted to pick up at the mall, the latest novel your book club is discussing that you haven't started reading yet, your dearest friend (the one you haven't called in weeks!), the diet you've been meaning to start.

> Our boast is this: the testimony of our conscience that we behaved in the world with simplicity and godly sincerity, not by earthly wisdom but by the grace of God.
>
> **2 Corinthians 1:12** ESV

11

So here's the question: how do you filter through all the demands *of* life so that you can focus on the essentials *for* life?

Jesus told his followers that even those who accepted his truth could end up living unproductive lives if they became "overwhelmed with worries about all the things they have to do and all the things they want to get. The stress strangles what they heard, and nothing comes of it" (Mark 4:19 MSG). People don't consciously neglect their relationship with God; they are simply distracted from fulfilling their purpose on earth one little to-do at a time. Jesus knew the people of his time needed to hear that, and he knows you need to hear it today.

You can't do everything, but you can figure out what is most important—what is essential—and put that first. Jesus said that if people would seek God above everything else and choose to live for him, then he would take care of everything else (Matthew 6:33).

The challenge, then, is to find those essentials, essentials such as knowing what you believe and why. How can you know God more deeply and please him more fully? How should you be living your life every day to make the most of what God has blessed you with? If you look first to these vital issues, you can be certain God will fill in all the other details. God promised that he will do his part if you will do yours. What a great deal!

Essentials for Life for Women will help you learn how to put first things first, live with confidence, and enjoy a fulfilled life. It will also help you discover how to live the best life you can possibly live by placing priority on the essentials.

Generosity

In a great trial of affliction the abundance of their joy and their deep poverty abounded in the riches of their liberality. For I bear witness that according to their ability, yes, and beyond their ability, they were freely willing, imploring us with much urgency that we would receive the gift and the fellowship of the ministering to the saints. And not only as we had hoped, but they first gave themselves to the Lord, and then to us by the will of God.

2 Corinthians 8:2–5 NKJV

No one has ever become poor by giving.

Anne Frank

Giving frees us from the familiar territory of our own needs by opening our mind to the unexplained worlds occupied by the needs of others.

Barbara Bush

Get to Know God, Your Creator

From Genesis to Revelation, the Bible reveals who God is—the powerful and mighty Creator, to be sure, but also the loving and merciful God who wants to have a relationship with every person on earth, and that includes you. He already knows you; it's time to get to know him.

When you respond to God's invitation to be in relationship with him, you begin to discover the depth of his love for you and the special purpose he has for your life. You realize that there's a reason you are alive in the world today, and that reason has everything to do with the fact that God is real, God is personal, and God cares about you. As your awareness of God's activity in your life grows, life itself takes on greater dimensions. Life becomes bigger—much more than simply surviving another crazy day.

In fact, part of God's purpose for your life is that you take your rightful place in a drama that has been unfolding since he created the first humans. This drama is the greatest love story of all time—

One of the areas that is particularly impacted by our view of God is our view of ourselves. If we do not see him as he really is—if we believe things about him that are not true—invariably, we will have a distorted view of ourselves.

Nancy Leigh DeMoss

not a story of earthly passion, but one of eternal purpose. God began to set the stage for this story when he created the earth and everything in it, all for the benefit of his crowning achievement, women and men. His purpose in creating the entire universe— including the galaxies, stars, nebula, quasars, planets, and even the rosemary you planted last week—was to share it with you. That's the extent of his love for you—it stretches all the way out to infinity.

Until you know through personal experience who God is, you will never truly know who you are.
—Darlene Zschech

This is the point of all creation: that you can know God as deeply and intimately as he knows you. As a woman, you know the value of intimate relationships—and you know they can't be forced. Genuine intimacy requires a willingness to invest in the relationship. God gives you that choice; you can choose if you want to be in a loving, intimate relationship with him. God's love is so great that he is willing to let you decide if you want to get to know him. He knows he risks losing you, but he also knows that a coerced relationship is no relationship at all. His gift to you is the freedom to choose.

Make no mistake about it, though—God continues to pursue those who reject him using any means he can. And one way is by placing reminders of his existence everywhere. His fingerprints

interesting to note

A New Zealand researcher set out to learn how God communicated to people through nature. After several days in the wilderness—and without any prompting—participants consistently said they felt as if God had created everything just for them.

are evident throughout the universe. A stunning sunset behind a snowcapped mountain range, waves crashing against a shoreline, the grandeur of a rugged canyon, and the simple eloquence of an apple orchard all depict the care God took in fashioning the earth. He made certain that creation reflected his artistry. When words fail to convince people of God's existence, the wonder and beauty of creation often win them over.

And God revealed himself in the Bible. In essence, he wrote a long letter describing his plan to break down the barriers that were keeping people from being in a relationship with him—or wanting to be in a relationship with him. In the Bible, God told about his efforts throughout early history to show his love and forgiveness to the very people who repeatedly rejected him. He told about sending Jesus to earth, and why it was necessary for him to die.

Jesus in turn revealed a great deal about God. He revealed how it was possible to follow God's plan and find joy in the process. He showed people that there was a much better way of living than what they were experiencing, that life was meant to be bigger—much more than simply surviving another crazy day, even in Jerusalem.

This is eternal life, that they may know You, the only true God, and Jesus Christ whom You have sent.

John 17:3 NKJV

Getting to know God is in some ways similar to the way you get to know another person. To discover more about him, spend time with him, read his "letter" (the Bible), and get together with people who love him and enjoy being in his presence.

what's essential

 God invites you to have a relationship with him. Respond to his invitation, and let him show you how much he loves you. Your relationship will grow according to the time and attention you give to him. Each day presents an opportunity for you to draw closer to him.

DO take steps to know God better by reading the Bible and discovering his fingerprints in creation.

DO show God how much you appreciate your freedom to choose by freely choosing to follow him.

DON'T miss the opportunity of a lifetime—the opportunity to personally experience God's love.

DON'T even consider living a "little" life ever again; let the dimensions of your life expand to accommodate God's activity.

Meet Jesus, the Son of God

Jesus is the link between heaven and earth. Through his ministry, sacrifice, and resurrection, the paradise that was lost in the garden of Eden was regained. Meeting Jesus is the most essential of all life's essentials, because getting to know Jesus is getting to know God. And that leads to a new way of living.

Jesus said this: "Whoever has seen me has seen the Father" (John 14:9 ESV). God chose to come to earth in human form to show his love and mercy and to repair the severed relationship between him and humanity. People who had been cold to the judgmental, condemning God portrayed by the religious leaders of their day discovered in Jesus a warmth and a compassion that better reflected God's true nature. For the first time, many people found a sense of worth in this man and his teachings. The poor, the downtrodden, the sick, and the outcast all flocked to him, along with one particular group that had been routinely dismissed and ignored—women.

Grace Eneme, an evangelical leader in Africa, put it this way: "Christ was the only rabbi who did not discriminate against women in his time." As a teacher, or rabbi, Jesus invited women to participate in his ministry. To other rabbis, that was scandalous. But Jesus had little use for those who had distorted God's message in an effort to build themselves up and tear everyone else down. He ignored the scandal.

Beloved, whatever we are gripping to bring us the satisfaction is a lie—unless it is Christ. He is the Truth that sets us free.
—Beth Moore

In Jesus, the people found a generous, welcoming spirit. Jesus gave them his time and attention, his wisdom and knowledge, his love and concern. And he gave them hope. For women, this meant, among other things, a release from the subordinate roles they had been forced to play. Jesus welcomed them into his circle of friends. He welcomed them as followers, as supporters, and as witnesses to his profound power. They watched as he healed the sick, the lame, the deaf, and the blind. They saw him restore the brokenhearted to a life of wholeness and joy. They witnessed his power to transform lives—including their own.

The gospel accounts of Matthew, Mark, Luke, and John tell the story of the life, ministry, and purpose of Jesus. His every action revealed God's original intentions for humanity. He provided a way for God once again to walk closely with his beloved creation. To this end, Jesus lived a life of quiet, devoted obscurity until he was thirty years old. He then went forth with a simple message: turn back to the God who loves you and will help you

He is the radiance of the glory of God and the exact imprint of his nature, and he upholds the universe by the word of his power. After making purification for sins, he sat down at the right hand of the Majesty on high.

Hebrews 1:3 ESV

live the abundant life. By the way he lived, Jesus demonstrated the kind of life God had intended for humanity all along.

But Jesus' teachings and way of living undermined the authority of the religious elite, who labeled him a rebel and a blasphemer. Blinded by their own selfish ambitions, the religious leaders failed to recognize him as Messiah and Son of God—God who had come to earth to restore his relationship with everyone, including them. Ironically, the very scriptures they quoted to accuse Jesus were those that proved he was the Messiah.

Threatened by his popularity, the religious elite ordered that Jesus be beaten and nailed to a cross to pay for crimes he did not commit: "He took the punishment . . . that made us whole" (Isaiah 53:5 MSG). His death on the cross eliminated the final barrier between God and humanity. Every person could finally enjoy a personal, intimate relationship with God.

And then, in a final, dramatic act, Jesus rose from the dead. Jesus conquered death. He is as alive today as he was when he walked on earth. And he promises this: that the same power that raised him from the dead is able to raise you up to a new life in relationship with him.

God wants a face-to-face, one-on-one relationship with us. He demonstrated that by sending Jesus to earth as a flesh-and-blood human whom other humans could relate to. He has made the first move in having a relationship with you. You can return the courtesy by getting to know him.

what's essential

 Through Jesus, God showed the magnitude of his love for us. Jesus lived a perfect life but made the ultimate sacrifice by dying as a criminal on a cross. That made it possible for us to live in the presence of God. All that is required of any of us is to accept that sacrifice.

DO read the gospel accounts to discover how Jesus modeled the abundant life for us.

DO imitate Jesus by developing a generous, welcoming spirit toward everyone.

DON'T depersonalize Jesus' death on the cross, but realize that he suffered and died for you.

DON'T ever forget Jesus' radical outreach to women, which is as active today as it was when he lived on earth.

Discover Jesus as Your Friend

Women instinctively know that relationships are one of the keys to living a joyful, fulfilled life. And there is no more important relationship in your life than the one you have with God through Jesus. Jesus goes so far as to describe himself as your friend. But what does it mean to be friends with Jesus?

No longer do I call you servants, for the servant does not know what his master is doing; but I have called you friends, for all that I have heard from my Father I have made known to you.

John 15:15 ESV

When you are rightly related to God, it is a life of freedom and liberty and delight, you are God's will, and all your commonsense decisions are His will for you unless He checks. You decide things in perfect delightful friendship with God.

Oswald Chambers

Think about your closest friends—the women with whom you laugh and cry, the women you love spending time with, the women who allow you to be yourself. Your closest friends are the women with whom you share your deepest feelings. Your hopes, fears, insecurities, questions—all that and more can be entrusted to a handful of friends, or perhaps just one friend, whose faithfulness has proven them to be trustworthy. The deeper the friendship, the fewer secrets you keep from one another.

Imagine having that kind of relationship with God. You can, through intimacy with Jesus. He called his followers "friends," because there was nothing he withheld from them (John 15:15). By not holding anything back from them, Jesus created a level of intimacy with his closest followers—his disciples—that elevated them to the status of friends. Psalm 84:11 assures us that God will not withhold any good thing from those who follow him and who live the kind of lives that bring joy to him. If that describes you, you are a friend of God.

 A rule I have had for years is: to treat the Lord Jesus Christ as a personal friend. His is not a creed, a mere doctrine, but it is He Himself we have.
—Dwight L. Moody

Deep friendships require deep communication. With God, deep communication comes more naturally than it might with a newfound friend. When you know that the one you're talking to—and listening to—already knows everything about you and everything about the universe and everything about everything, the challenge becomes less one of trust and more one of figuring out what on earth to say to him. Since he already knows your deepest secrets, you may feel foolish talking to him about them. Relax. Yes, he's the all-knowing Creator, but he's also your friend, and he wants to hear you express your thoughts in your own words, straight from your own heart. If it helps, visualize Jesus sitting with you, his eyes riveted on you as you share your innermost feelings.

Jesus wants to be that kind of friend to you, someone you can talk with about anything and everything. He also wants to be a friend you can lean on in difficult times. And he wants to be a friend you can trust not only with your secrets but also with the desires of your heart. You know you've reached a new level of

trust when you begin to share your desires with him and believe he wants to fulfill them. You actually start to have faith that what you ask for, you will receive (Matthew 7:7). On that deeper level, you begin to recognize how lavish God is with the gifts he gives his friends, his followers.

You deepen your friendship with God by reading about his life, meditating on his sayings, and talking things over with him in prayer. And you learn to "practice his presence" throughout the day by intentionally turning your thoughts toward him and consciously sensing his presence with you, no matter what you are doing. You sense him there beside you whether you are cleaning the house, volunteering at an animal shelter, or checking items off your to-do list at work. When a crisis hits, you *know* he is there. You never have to question that. But even if you don't sense his presence, he is there.

The more time you spend with him, the more clearly you recognize the things he wants you to do. He may ask you to reach out to the person in the next cubicle whose marriage is falling apart, or support an orphaned child in another country with your love and finances, or give your time to an organization working to end human rights abuses. As you respond to his desires, his concerns become your concerns—and your friendship with God reaches an even deeper level.

Jesus called you to be his friend because he wants you to share your joys and heartaches with him. He seeks friends he can work alongside to bring hope to the world. If you find yourself concerned about the things that concern Jesus, you can delight in a friendship with him.

what's essential

 When he was on earth, Jesus sought out people who wanted to walk with him every day and share his mission and purpose. He does the same today. Those who share his vision for a life of purpose and live it out on a daily basis are those who have the right to call themselves his friends.

DO begin to see Jesus as a friend with whom you can share your deepest thoughts.

DO believe that God wants to give lavishly to those he calls his friends.

DON'T take your friendship with Jesus so casually that you overlook the fact that he is still the Son of God.

DON'T forget that friendship requires communication, and with God that means spending time in prayer.

Experience the Holy Spirit, God's Presence

When Jesus left the earth, the Holy Spirit was sent to offer guidance, direction, and comfort and to help anyone who believed that Jesus was the Son of God. In essence, the Spirit is God's active presence on earth. He is the power source that enables God's people to accomplish what God wants them to.

At the Last Supper, Jesus talked about the one who would come after he left for heaven, the Holy Spirit—the third member of the Trinity, along with God the Father and God the Son. The Trinity is a difficult concept for even biblical scholars to comprehend and explain, but what's essential is that you understand that the Holy Spirit is God, and he lives inside those who follow God wholeheartedly, providing those who love him with a continual connection to his power and wisdom.

In ancient times, the Israelites thought of God's Spirit in feminine terms, and recent decades have seen a return to this understanding. The common

Christian view, however, is that God contains both male and female attributes. Still, many women who are followers of Jesus find they readily gravitate to the Holy Spirit because the Bible never depicts the Holy Spirit in masculine terms. Most translations do use masculine pronouns to refer to the Spirit, but unlike God the Father and Jesus the Son, the Holy Spirit is free of any concrete association with either gender. It's easier for some women, particularly those who have suffered at the hands of men, to relate to the gender-free image of the Holy Spirit.

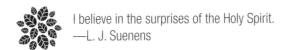 I believe in the surprises of the Holy Spirit.
—L. J. Suenens

And then there's this passage in the Old Testament book of Joel: "I will pour out my Spirit on all people. Your sons and daughters will prophesy, your old men will dream dreams, your young men will see visions. Even on my servants, both men and women, I will pour out my Spirit" (2:28–29 NIV). Women who have been denied the opportunity to serve God in ministry positions have found both comfort and validity in their assurance that God does indeed pour out his Spirit on women as well as men.

But the most powerful connection between the Holy Spirit and a woman is found in Matthew's account of the birth of Jesus. Matthew stated the fact in a most straightforward way. The unmarried and virginal Mary, he wrote, "was found to be with child through the Holy Spirit" (Matthew 1:18 NIV). As astonishing as that news was, Matthew offered no further explanation.

I tell you that I am going to do what is best for you. That is why I am going away. The Holy Spirit cannot come to help you until I leave.

John 16:7 CEV

Soon enough, though, an angel of God appeared to Joseph, who had second thoughts about marrying Mary when he discovered that she was pregnant. The angel told him, "Do not be afraid to take Mary home as your wife, because what is conceived in her is from the Holy Spirit" (Matthew 1:20 NIV).

It's no wonder that women of today sense a special connection with the Holy Spirit; the Spirit, who could have produced Jesus out of thin air, instead set an ordinary young woman apart for special distinction by choosing her to nurture the Son of God in her womb and give birth to him at the appointed time.

Women—and men—of today experience the presence of the Holy Spirit in a variety of ways: as one who teaches (John 14:26), reveals what is true (John 16:13), leads God's people (Romans 8:14), strengthens them in their weakness (Romans 8:26), and prays in their place when they don't know how to pray (Romans 8:26).

The Holy Spirit will help you develop spiritual strength and learn how to live a life that is pleasing to God. If you begin to veer off course, he will gently remind you of the words of Jesus and the wisdom of God, nudge you with a quiet uneasiness about the situation you find yourself in, or impress your conscience with a strong feeling that things aren't quite right.

The Holy Spirit enables you to accomplish everything God wants you to do. As you encounter obstacles, the Spirit shores you up and gives you the strength and courage to go on. Best of all, you can have the assurance that he will always be with you, no matter how rough the going gets.

what's essential

 God sent the Holy Spirit to help you understand the Bible, discern his voice, grow in his personality traits, give you strength when you are weak, and guide you as you seek God's desires for your life.

DO learn who the Holy Spirit is and how to follow his leading.

DO trust the Spirit to give you the ability to accomplish whatever God asks of you.

DON'T let your questions about the Trinity interfere with your relationship with the Holy Spirit.

DON'T limit the work of the Holy Spirit in your life by resisting his leading.

Understanding God's Goodness

The way you envision God—in terms of his activity on earth and his interaction with his people—plays a significant role in your interaction with him. Recognizing the goodness in his actions and his thoughts toward you will go a long way toward ensuring that you have a strong and healthy relationship with him.

I know the thoughts that I think toward you, says the LORD, thoughts of peace and not of evil, to give you a future and a hope.

Jeremiah 29:11 NKJV

O ne of the most important things you need to know about God is that he is good. Look at all he created for humanity—the earth and everything in it was created for our benefit and pleasure. The garden of Eden was a paradise, a perfect place where, according to the Bible, the first people walked and talked with God in the cool of the evening. What a picture of his goodness!

Even after those first people showed their disrespect for him by failing to do what he asked, God left much of the goodness of creation intact. Consider the variety of colors in a field of flowers, the fragrance of a pine forest after the rain, the sound of water tumbling over smooth rocks in a clear mountain stream, the taste of everything from the spiciest chili pepper to the sweetest piece

If you feel stuck, bring your whole self to Christ, not just the problem, but you. Ask God to change your heart. Commit yourself to pray to that end. It's God's heart to give good gifts to His children.

Sheila Walsh

of melt-in-your-mouth chocolate. It may not be paradise, but this post-Eden world boasts countless evidences of the goodness of God.

 Our circumstances are not an accurate reflection of God's goodness. Whether life is good or bad, God's goodness, rooted in His character, is the same.
—Helen Grace Lescheid

His goodness, of course, extends beyond the natural world and into the spiritual realm. From the beginning of his ministry, Jesus placed one message front and center: the kingdom of God would be coming soon. For Jews living under an oppressive Roman government, this was good news indeed. God would intervene, oust the Romans from power, and restore the region of Palestine—including present-day Israel—to its rightful owners, the people of God. Those who believed in the message that Jesus preached were certain that they knew who their next king would be. That king would be Jesus, and all would be right with the world once again.

What they didn't understand was that the kingdom of God was not a political structure like that which they were accustomed to in the natural world. As Jesus defined it, the kingdom of God was in God's people and all around them. It existed wherever there was peace, joy, and *righteousness*—another word for *virtue* or *morality*. It was a place where the paralyzed could walk, the blind could see, and the sick could be healed. In essence, it was a place where the ultimate good—God—would reign.

The ultimate good, though, wasn't good enough for some of the people. They wanted an earthly king, and when Jesus failed to fill that bill, they wanted nothing more to do with him. But those who continued to follow him to the cross and beyond had their eyes opened to the truth about the kingdom of God because, suddenly, they were experiencing that peace, joy, and righteousness. Suddenly, when they prayed for the paralyzed, the blind, and the sick, those people were being healed—even though Jesus had gone to be with God the Father! *That* was the kingdom of God at work, and it was all good.

The kingdom of God is a spiritual realm in which God's goodness makes itself evident to his people. Staying up all night with a friend who just lost her mother is God's goodness at work through you. Sending a meal to a family with a new baby is God's goodness at work through you as well. And being on the receiving end of things that have been a blessing to your life is the kingdom of God and his goodness working on your behalf.

Always remember that what God wants for you is good. He wants you to know that his plans for you include "a future and a hope" (Jeremiah 29:11 NKJV)—a fulfilling, joyful, peaceful life.

We know that God is always at work for the good of everyone who loves him.

Romans 8:28 CEV

Train yourself to be aware of the kingdom of God in your life. Look for evidences of his goodness. As you get into that habit, you'll discover the abundance of good things that God has brought into your everyday life.

what's essential

 God's kingdom—his invisible work on earth through and for his people—is a kingdom of goodness. Understanding that God is good gives you a healthy perspective on your relationship with him, one that will serve you well throughout your life.

DO expect God to bring good things into your life.

DO be aware that the kingdom of God is constantly working on your behalf.

DON'T become so focused on things that go wrong in the world that you overlook evidence of God's goodness.

DON'T forget that the kingdom of God works not just for you but also through you.

Adversity

All praise to the God and Father of our Master, Jesus the Messiah! Father of all mercy! God of all healing counsel! He comes alongside us when we go through hard times, and before you know it, he brings us alongside someone else who is going through hard times so that we can be there for that person just as God was there for us. We have plenty of hard times that come from following the Messiah, but no more so than the good times of his healing comfort—we get a full measure of that, too.

2 Corinthians 1:3–5 MSG

Often, in the midst of great problems, we stop short of the real blessing God has for us, which is a fresh vision of who He is.

Anne Graham Lotz

Pain is inevitable. Suffering is optional.

M. Kathleen Casey

Know God's Word, the Bible

The Bible is the top-selling book of all time; no other book even comes close to the Bible in terms of sales. But more important than that is the impact it has had on the world—and its impact on the world of women simply can't be overstated. Knowing what the Bible has to say is essential for any woman who wants to have a deeper relationship with God.

If you haven't read the Bible in a while—or ever—you're in for a treat when you do. Many people think they are familiar with the contents of the Bible, but what they are actually familiar with is what other people have told them about it. When they open the pages of this remarkable book and begin to read it for themselves, they are often pleasantly surprised at what they discover on those pages. And you know what? People who have read the Bible regularly for years often find that they, too, are pleasantly surprised, because passages that they've read many times in the past suddenly come to life with new meaning and great relevance to their lives at that moment.

All Scripture is given by inspiration of God, and is profitable for doctrine, for reproof, for correction, for instruction in righteousness, that the man of God may be complete, thoroughly equipped for every good work.

2 Timothy 3:16–17
NKJV

I want to know one thing: the way to heaven. God himself has condescended to teach me the way. He has written it down in a book. Oh, give me that book! At any price give me the book of God.

John Wesley

There's no question. The Bible is a literary masterpiece that stands alone among the sacred writings of the world's major religions. Many scholars see it as just that and nothing more. But it is more than that—much more. Among Christians, the Bible is often called the Word of God, signifying the belief that God conveyed his message to humanity through the forty or so authors who contributed to the writing of the Bible. The sixty-six books that are contained in the Bible don't reflect the thoughts and opinions of mere mortals; they reflect the heart of the eternal God.

There is no rupture but [rather] continuity between what was revealed to the people of God in the past and the breath of the Spirit that accompanies the reading of the Bible in faith communities today.
—Tereza Cavalcanti

For women, the Bible reveals that the heart of the eternal God beats with love and respect for them. The Bible records stories about women who were able to influence their culture even in an ancient patriarchal society. In the pages of the Bible you can read about Deborah, a wise prophet and judge who saved the Israelites from further oppression; and Esther, a queen who risked her own life to keep her people from certain annihilation. Those and other accounts of influential women in biblical times have offered hope and encouragement to women for two millennia and counting.

Most important, though, is the fact that the Bible is God's personal letter to you. He wrote it so you would know how to find him—how to connect with him, how to follow and imitate him, and how to walk in his wisdom. The Bible contains thousands of promises for those who put their trust in him, principles for living a productive and successful life, and stories about God's intervention that will encourage you to trust him even more. History, poetry, memoirs, letters, prophecy—it's all there just waiting to be read.

Look at a few things the Bible says about itself:

- *The Bible is eternal.* "The grass withers, the flower fades, but the word of our God will stand forever" (Isaiah 40:8 ESV).

- *The Bible truly is the Word of God.* "Everything in the Scriptures is God's Word. All of it is useful for teaching and helping people and for correcting them and showing them how to live" (2 Timothy 3:16 CEV).

- *The Bible is a living, dynamic document.* "The word of God is alive and powerful" (Hebrews 4:12 NLT).

As you become reacquainted with the Bible, ask God how you can apply its ancient teachings to your own twenty-first-century life. Remember that the Bible is the eternal, living, dynamic Word of God, and that means it is timeless and relevant even

interesting to note

The eighteenth-century French philosopher Voltaire predicted that within a century of his death, the Bible would be "eliminated" and replaced by his own writings. He died in 1778, and the Bible remains a perennial best seller. Today, most of Voltaire's writings are primarily of interest to philosophers and academics.

You need to realize that no one alone can understand any of the prophecies in the Scriptures. The prophets did not think these things up on their own, but they were guided by the Spirit of God.

2 Peter 1:20–21 CEV

today. Its powerful words transcend time and space. A career-oriented woman in Massachusetts, an oppressed and fearful mother in Afghanistan, an older woman anywhere who must suddenly care for grandchildren abandoned by their parents—every woman in every circumstance can find hope and strength in the pages of the Bible.

One of the best ways to get to know God is to regularly read his message to the world. Daily schedules for reading the Bible can be found online and in bookstores. You may even discover one tucked away in the back pages of your own Bible.

what's essential

 The Bible is a source of comfort in times of trouble and a song of praise in times of victory. Its wisdom and relevance are timeless.

DO read the Bible from a fresh perspective, no matter how familiar you are with its message.

DO take the Bible personally—God intends it to speak to your life today.

DON'T just read the Bible, but study it and put it into practice in your life.

DON'T lock Scripture into one interpretation only, but ask God to reveal to you its deeper meanings each time you read it.

Live as If Heaven Is Home

If you're looking forward to going to heaven someday, there's great news for you in the here and now. Eternal life isn't something you experience only after you die, because eternity—being timeless—can't be confined to the afterlife. It's here, it's now, and it's just like having heaven on earth.

> If they had been talking about the land where they had once lived, they could have gone back at any time. But they were looking forward to a better home in heaven.
>
> **Hebrews 11:15–16** CEV

When life threatens to overwhelm you, it's only natural that you want to escape it, and for many people that escape means the hope of going to heaven. When life is going well and you've become comfortable with the routines and rhythm of the culture around you, you may think that you can hold off on going to heaven for a while. Whether things are going downhill or uphill for you, you need to remember that this world isn't your ultimate home—heaven is. But that doesn't mean you can't bring a bit of heaven into your life today.

When you enter into a relationship with God, you experience both a present reality—the kingdom of God and all the good things that go with

> His message was simple and austere, like his desert surroundings: "Change your life. God's kingdom is here."
>
> **Matthew 3:2** MSG

39

it—and the future hope of heaven. You are no longer a citizen of this world trying to work your way into heaven. You are a citizen of heaven making your way through this world and trying to pick up as many traveling companions as you can along the way. Even though your citizenship is in heaven, however, you're still living on earth. And that creates a tension: you know you should appreciate life on earth, but you long for heaven.

The answer—or rather, one answer—to easing that tension is to grab hold of what you understand about heaven and apply it to your life on earth.

 If I find in myself a desire which no experience in this world can satisfy, the most probable explanation is that I was made for another world.
—C. S. Lewis

Wrapping your head around that notion may be easier if you think in terms of worldwide travel. Imagine that you and a friend travel to Beijing for an extended visit and become immersed in Chinese culture. You notice the language, the unfamiliar food available in stores and restaurants, the appropriate way to haggle at open-air markets, and a host of customs that define proper Chinese etiquette. It's exciting but also bewildering; you want so much to go home and be with those you love. But it's not time yet. You and your friend decide to bring a little bit of home to Beijing by hunting down foods from your country and inviting your newfound Chinese friends over for a taste of your home culture. You talk about your country and answer one question after another about *home*—your real home. You bring the heart and soul of your home into another country.

You can do that here and now. You can bring the heart and soul of heaven into your work, your family, your friendships, and the routines and rhythms of your everyday life. You do that by re-membering that while you are on earth, you are living in the kingdom of God—heaven on earth. As you share God's goodness and blessings with other people, you are giving them a taste of the kingdom of God and the kingdom of heaven.

While this may help you navigate your way through this life, it doesn't necessarily make things easy. You are still in this world, and you will experience trouble and hardships, even though you are a citizen of a different kingdom. But that's even more reason to cling to your relationship with God, who wants you to grasp the fact that you can glimpse eternity and live as if heaven is home even though you are confined to a certain time and space on earth.

Because you belong to heaven, you have a hope that overpowers you in whatever circumstances

interesting to note

In Matthew, Mark, and Luke, the central themes of Jesus' teachings were the kingdom of God and the kingdom of heaven. John, however, used the term *eternal life* to describe the focus of Jesus' teaching. John defined *eternal life* as "knowing God" (John 17:3).

The doctrine of the Kingdom of Heaven, which was the main teaching of Jesus, is certainly one of the most revolutionary doctrines that ever stirred and changed human thought.

H. G. Wells

you find yourself. There is another world to look forward to. You were ultimately meant for something better, a place "whose designer and builder is God" (Hebrews 11:10 ESV).

The blessings of heaven come from being in God's presence. You can experience "heaven on earth" by welcoming God into every area of your life.

what's essential

 Let heaven be a source of hope for you and for those whose lives you touch.

DO appreciate both life on earth and the life that is to come in heaven.

DO allow your understanding of heaven to affect your everyday life and the way you act toward others.

DON'T look at going to heaven as an escape from this world, but find ways to bring the hope of heaven into this world.

DON'T let the time and space restrictions on earth prevent you from living as if heaven is your home.

Trust God

God wants you to trust him more and more each day, but sometimes it feels as if he's asking you to trust him for the impossible. God has promised, however, to help you accomplish—and endure— whatever he asks you to do. Every time you trust him in a given situation, you learn just how trustworthy he is.

An Ohio State University study confirmed what women already knew—that women are most likely to develop long-lasting, trusting relationships with people they've met through close friends and family members. Membership in an organization of like-minded women isn't enough. Without a close, personal connection, trusting relationships take longer to establish.

Think about how you came into a relationship with God. It's highly likely that a friend or relative you trust was instrumental in introducing you to God. It's even possible that you once attended church but never made a real connection with God there—because associating with like-minded

Trust in him at all times, O people; pour out your heart before him; God is a refuge for us.

Psalm 62:8 ESV

God will never, never, never let us down if we have faith and put our trust in Him. He will always look after us. So we must cleave to Jesus. Our whole life must simply be woven into Jesus.

Mother Teresa

people wasn't enough for you. It took trusting a friend who trusted God to open you up to trusting God for yourself.

 A woman of true beauty is a woman who in the depths of her soul is at rest, trusting God because she has come to know him to be worthy of her trust.
—Stasi Eldredge

When you first come into a relationship with God, you may believe that you have placed all your faith in him—and for a while, that's probably true. But a life of faith is a journey, and you never know what's up ahead until you get there. That's when the issue of trust may become more difficult. Say you have an opportunity to take a job in a field you love, but it comes with a significant pay cut. God seems to be nudging you in that direction, but you have a mortgage payment that depends on your current salary. This is the first time God has placed such a difficult decision before you, but it's possible that he has done so in order to show you that you can trust him with difficult decisions. He wants to prove to you just how trustworthy he is.

As with friendships, a deep trust in God develops over time. At the start of your relationship, you may trust God for things that aren't likely to happen without his intervention—your stubborn '95 minivan starting on the first try, for example—but also aren't impossible. As you trust God for bigger and bigger things, you "grow in faith," a phrase that describes your maturing trust in God. As you continue to trust him for the nearly impossible, you come closer to that time when he will ask you to trust him for the impossible.

That's the moment when you learn what trust really is. Don't be surprised if the impossible thing he's asking you to do is also a very public thing.

George Mueller's trust in God was tested to the limit in a highly visible setting. He operated a number of orphanages in nineteenth-century England, housing some two thousand children at one point. He was roundly criticized for giving unfair advantage to the poor, and his ministry to the children came under scrutiny. His refusal to ask for donations was well known, and more than once there was no food in the pantry to prepare the orphans' next meal. But he'd have the children take their places at the tables anyway, totally confident that God would not allow them to go hungry. And God always came through. Whatever the children needed arrived at the door at just the right time.

Imagine being in that position. All eyes are on you, just waiting for you to make some big blunder, like letting two thousand children you claim to love go without nourishment. The temptation today would be to whip out the credit card or send out a tearful plea to donors. But if that's not what God wants you to do, then the alternative is to trust him with something so big and so public that you would face utter humiliation and ridicule if he didn't come through.

interesting to note

Batach, a Hebrew verb meaning "to trust," carries with it the connotation of being careless— or being without a care. The idea is that those who trust in someone or something feel safe and secure. That's what God wants for you—to trust him on such a deep level that you feel safe, secure, and free of worry.

Give all your worries and cares to God, for he cares about you.

1 Peter 5:7 NLT

Trust builds on trust. Trust God with the little things, and then the medium things, and then the big things. Soon enough, you'll be trusting him with the impossible things.

Think about the things you've been trusting God for. If they're too "easy," it may be time to trust God with something bigger. What is it that you desperately want to see happen in your life? If you think it's something God would be pleased to provide for you, trust him to do so.

what's essential

 Trusting God is essential to having a close, loving relationship with him. Only by trusting him can you claim to be a true follower of God.

DO recognize the importance of trusting God with everything in your life.

DO realize that you are on a faith journey and don't know what you may need to trust God for in the future.

DON'T have any expectations about how God will provide for you, but allow him to surprise you with whatever he has for you.

DON'T forget the times God has come through for you in the past.

Know How to Talk About Jesus

It is not unusual for people to feel a little wary of sharing their faith. That needn't be the case, however. You don't have to be a great preacher or a seasoned evangelist or a Bible scholar to talk to others about God. You just have to be yourself.

Talking to people about God can be intimidating for a multitude of reasons. You know you don't have all the answers, but what if they think you should? You've probably heard someone else talk about God so effortlessly that you may be embarrassed at how hard it is for you to do the same. Or maybe you've been part of conversations about God that left someone feeling offended—possibly even you. All that messes with your head, and you start to think, *I just can't do this.*

Those feelings of inadequacy and memories of failed attempts at talking to others about God can leave you paralyzed. But paralysis is nothing to God. He's the great healer of the paralyzed! Give him your fears and your bad memories, and he'll get you moving again. Take a deep breath, return

Sanctify the Lord God in your hearts, and always be ready to give a defense to everyone who asks you a reason for the hope that is in you, with meekness and fear.

1 Peter 3:15 NKJV

Christ has placed me on this planet to leave a legacy and message of hope. The Lord's life-saving truth isn't meant to be held close, but to be extended. He wants our lives to become an offering.

Nichole Nordeman

to square one, and decide that you can effortlessly share your faith with anyone at any appropriate time, as long as you keep three things in mind: you don't need to know it all, you don't need to be anyone but yourself, and you don't need to listen to any voice in your head except the voice of the Holy Spirit.

 If you teach men that God is the source of their pleasure and sin is the source of their pain, they will run to God and away from sin.
—Jacquelyn K. Heasley

As you read the Gospels, you realize that people flocked to Jesus because someone else told them about his teaching or a miracle he performed or, very likely, the way he really gave it to the arrogant religious leaders at that time. Imagine yourself living in Jerusalem in the first century. Jesus has just healed your brother of leprosy. What would you do? You would rush from one house to the next, blurting out the good news to all the women in the village, urging them to go with you to hear this incredible man talk about things like the kingdom of God and how he has come to bring hope—to bring God—to ordinary people! Telling your friends about Jesus would be the easiest thing in the world, because your words would flow from a heart filled with wonder and joy and gratitude. That's how you share your faith.

If there's ever a time when you should speak from your heart, this is it—a time when you feel it's the right time to ease the subject of God and your faith in him into a conversation. Often that time comes when you sense a deep need in the life of someone you're talking to, and you know that only God can meet that need. If the Holy Spirit is prompting you to speak up, then you can count on the Spirit to give you the words that will bring comfort and hope to your friend.

Remember, too, that by living fully and joyfully in the presence of others, you will show them by example what a relationship with Jesus can be like. Sprinkle your conversation with God's wisdom. Talk about the things you have discovered in your Bible reading. Tell others about your relationship with God the way you would tell them about any other relationship in your life.

Pray for friends and colleagues who need God's love. Ask God to let you know just what they need to hear. Pray that God will bring people into their lives who will also show them God's hope in word and action. Just as you trust God to lead you in other areas, also trust him to lead you in sharing him with the people around you.

Above all, love them. Show them God's love. And then just be yourself—someone who may not know it all but who can point the way to the one who does.

interesting to note

Here's a fascinating way to talk about God; it's the brainchild of two European missionaries. As they rode the subway, one would start telling the other—who played the role of a skeptic—about God. Without fail, other subway riders would get involved, resulting in an animated, public conversation about faith.

If you confess with your mouth, "Jesus is Lord," and believe in your heart that God raised him from the dead, you will be saved.

Romans 10:9 NIV

Just as prayer should be a foundation for every other area of your life, it should also be the foundation for preparing you to share with others what Jesus has done in your life. Pray daily for others, and be open for God to use you in answer to those prayers.

what's essential

 Be yourself. Share what you know and what you've experienced in your relationship with God. Follow the leading of the Holy Spirit. And relax. You'll do fine.

DO depend on God to help you talk to others about him.

DO speak from your heart, ignoring the pressure you may feel to get everything just right.

DON'T feel that you need to have the answer to every potential question before you can talk to others about your faith.

DON'T compare yourself with preachers, evangelists, or public speakers when it comes to your ability to tell your friends about God.

Be Confident to the End

Speculation about the end of the world is nothing new. For millennia, religious prognosticators have looked for signs that the end is near. But end-times theories are not confined to those with a spiritual bent. Today, predictions about everything from the threat of climate change to the future of the planet have brought the issue into the homes of even the nonreligious.

For many women, concerns about the end times—the end of the world and, for Christians, the return of Jesus to earth—have taken a backseat to the daily demands of their lives. Certainly Christian women have studied the many biblical prophecies that seem to indicate "the end is near," but in many cases daily demands have shifted their attention away from all but the most immediate concerns.

Many end-times discussions involve pinpointing the date of the return of Jesus, but women familiar with Matthew 24:36 know those predictions are pointless. That verse reads: "Of that day and hour no one knows, not even the angels of heaven, but My Father only" (NKJV). Remember the huge Y2K scare? Some financial prophets restricted their predictions to a massive banking failure, but some religious forecasters saw the turn of the second millennium in AD 2000 as a sign of Jesus' imminent return. But then, so did religious prophets at the turn of the first millennium in AD 1000. Many who feared that the end would come at the dawn of the twenty-first century breathed a sigh of relief, but their relief didn't last long.

 What the caterpillar calls the end of the world, the master calls a butterfly.
—Richard Bach

Between the escalating talk of climate change and the 9/11 attacks on the U.S., women have begun to look at end-times prophecies from several different perspectives—many of them highly personal. Will climate change so drastically alter the planet that there will be no future on earth for their children or their children's children? It doesn't matter whether these women are mothers or not; even women without children voice concerns about this, with some choosing not to have children because of these predictions.

When the 9/11 attacks led to war in the Middle East, Christian women began taking another look at biblical prophecies about Armageddon, the last great battle between God and his opponents. The site of the prophesied battle is in Israel, and every conflict in the Middle East in some way relates to Israel. As they have watched their boyfriends, husbands, sons, other significant men and even women in their lives leave to fight in Iraq and Afghanistan, some women have wondered if their loved ones were heading off to witness earth's horrifying finale.

Those who turn to the Bible for comfort and guidance may continue reading Matthew 24, where they discover that Jesus didn't finish his end-times discussion with verse 36. He continued by telling a parable about a faithful servant whose master went on an extended journey. Each day while his master was gone, this servant cared for the household as if his master would be returning the next day. Jesus contrasted him with a lazy servant who decided his master would never return and used his master's wealth and property for his own benefit. Of the two, Jesus asked, "Who then is the faithful and wise servant, whom his master has set over his household, to give them their food at the proper time? Blessed is that servant whom his master will find so doing when he comes" (Matthew 24:45–46 ESV).

This is the true intention of the biblical prophecies regarding the end times: people should continue to tend to those things that the master, God, has entrusted into their care—namely, the earth and all that is in it, including other people. Life is to go on as usual, with the understanding that Jesus could return at any time—creating an attitude of anticipation that says, "Hurry, let's do what the master has told us to do, so we will all be ready for his return!"

interesting to note

The most significant fulfillment of prophecy in the last century was the rebirth of the State of Israel in 1948. Many saw this as a sign that the end times were near, based on biblical passages that they believe link the Jews' return to Israel with Jesus' return to earth.

In My Father's house are many mansions . . . I go to prepare a place for you. And if I go and prepare a place for you, I will come again and receive you to Myself; that where I am, there you may be also.

John 14:2–3 NKJV

Those who have a narrow escape from death often find that they have a heightened sense of appreciation for every moment they live from that day forward. That's a good way to live, whether you believe that the earth's end—or your own end—is near or not.

what's essential

 It's pointless to speculate on an end-times schedule. Only God knows what the future holds. The essential thing to remember is that God has given you this life, and he wants you to live it to the fullest—taking care of all that he has entrusted to you the way you would if you knew Jesus was returning tomorrow.

DO live your life in joyful anticipation of whatever the future holds.

DO take special care of those things that God has entrusted to you.

DON'T try to predict or pay attention to predictions about the time and date of the end of the earth.

DON'T let the fear of end-times prophecies rob you of the peace that comes with knowing God has the future under control.

Trust

Jesus shouted to the crowds, "If you trust me, you are trusting not only me, but also God who sent me. For when you see me, you are seeing the one who sent me. I have come as a light to shine in this dark world, so that all who put their trust in me will no longer remain in the dark.

John 12:44–46 NLT

But now having seen him which is invisible I fear not what man can do unto me.

Anne Hutchinson

When a train goes through a tunnel and it gets dark, you don't throw away the ticket and jump off. You sit still and trust the engineer.

Corrie ten Boom

Read What God Wrote to You

Regularly reading the Bible as if it were personally written to you is one of the best ways to learn about God and understand how to relate to him. God still speaks and guides anew through the words of the Bible today—even in verses you have read many times before.

Have you ever had a loved one who was in a faraway place where it was too expensive to telephone regularly and Internet access was difficult? Perhaps as a young girl you were at camp and missed being home with your family and friends. You would wait for the mail every day, hoping there was something in it for you; or you spent a good deal of time writing letters yourself. When you received a letter, you would read it again and again, and even carry it with you so that you had it when you needed it the most.

This is really what God intended the Bible to be for you—a series of letters from someone who loves you very much and wants to be with you. It contains God's best advice for how to live on this

For some years now I have read through the Bible twice every year. If you picture the Bible to be a mighty tree and every word a little branch, I have shaken every one of these branches because I wanted to know what it was and what it meant.

Martin Luther

planet as well as how to know him and understand his ways. It holds the keys to plugging into his purposes and living a life filled with meaning.

 The Bible is to me the most precious thing in the world just because it tells me the story of Jesus.
—George MacDonald

Yet it is more than that as well. Jesus said, "Man shall not live by bread alone, but by every word that proceeds from the mouth of God" (Matthew 4:4 NKJV). In this sense, he likened the words of Scripture to food—spiritual food, if you will—and said that you need to be taking in God's words just as much as you need your next meal. The Bible is the source of spiritual stamina just as natural food is the source of physical stamina. It plants the seeds within you that grow into what the Bible calls the "fruit of the Spirit"—love, joy, peace, patience, kindness, goodness, faithfulness, gentleness, and self-control (Galatians 5:22–23)—and helps to prune things out of your life that hinder the growth of that fruit. It opens your eyes to truth in a way that frees you from the things that pull you down, such as jealousy, immorality, anger, hurt, and strife. Regularly reading the Bible keeps you from being spiritually weak in the midst of stress and temptation. It is what builds into you the strength of character and will to be successful in becoming the person you want to be rather than someone ruled by desires and impulses. If you were facing a long, hard, and grueling day, it's unlikely that you would skip

interesting to note

In earlier times, many people read the entire Bible each year. Catherine Booth, who with her husband, William, founded the Salvation Army, was a particularly avid Bible student. She read the entire Bible eight times—before she reached the age of twelve.

The Bereans were of more noble character than the Thessalonians, for they received the message with great eagerness and examined the Scriptures every day to see if what Paul said was true.

Acts 17:11 NIV

eating that day; you would want to be in top shape mentally and physically, and you would need nourishment to get you there. By making sure you don't skip your spiritual meals, you are spiritually prepared to face whatever the day holds for you.

As you read the Bible, you'll discover how frequently it offers insights and answers that can turn a situation around in an instant. As you go through your day and encounter troubling or confusing situations, a Bible passage you perused that morning or the night before may pop into your mind and turn out to provide just what you need to bring clarity to your circumstances.

Not only that, but as you read the Bible, God will reveal through his Holy Spirit some new aspect of a story or verse you may have read a hundred times—and that new perspective will bring a key insight into something you are facing. It will help you reach the right decision, give you the right thing to say, or give you the wisdom to avoid saying something you'll regret later. It will build into you the perseverance to see a situation through and develop the strength of love you need to reach out to others. Stay filled—with the Bible.

The wisdom and strength gained from daily Bible reading is something you have to experience to appreciate. Spend a week reading the Bible every day and see how it has an impact on your life. It truly is one of the essential elements in keeping alive your relationship with God.

what's essential

 A single bit of knowledge or wisdom that you glean from your Bible reading can transform a situation that's been bothering you for years. You can count on the words of the Bible to nourish you and strengthen you for the unknown circumstances you'll face each day.

DO view the Bible as spiritual food that is essential to the health of your spiritual life.

DO get in the habit of reading the Bible on a regular basis.

DON'T forget to pay attention to what God has to say to you through the Holy Spirit as you read the Bible.

DON'T skip your spiritual meal—your daily Bible reading—since you need the strength it offers throughout the day.

Seek God Through Prayer

In essence, prayer is simply an ongoing conversation with God that involves talking with him and actively listening for his response. But it is also much more than that—because a single prayer contains life-giving and life-changing power. It's an essential means of getting to know God better and enjoying time in his presence.

Prayer is the place where faith in God becomes practical. Prayer is your connection between heaven and the things of this earth. You talk to God in prayer about what he has planned for you and ask that his plans be fulfilled in your life and the lives of those around you. Prayer is your personal point of contact with God, and because of that, it can be both rewarding and difficult. What makes it difficult? Well, like many deep conversations you have with someone you care about, it takes time and focus. When you make a point of regularly taking time to talk to God—and try to keep stray thoughts from distracting your attention—you'll find that your time in prayer is time well spent.

Praying is a way of being with someone I know loves me.

Saint Teresa of Avila

It takes intentional effort to keep prayer from getting lost in the normal responsibilities and routines of everyday life.

That's especially true for you as a woman. It's all too easy to allow prayer to take a backseat to the other demands on your day. There's always one more thing that needs to be done. Knowing that—knowing you could work twenty-four/seven and still find that several other projects are vying for your attention—actually gives you a reason to stop what you're doing and have a conversation with God. When you realize you can't possibly get it all done, you have the freedom to let it all go. That frees you to turn your time and attention to God.

 There is something in the female, in her need for love and to give love, that comes out in the silent, compassionate awareness of prayer.
—Mother Mary Clare

The practice of prayer is about going before God with your concerns and laying them at his feet. It is also about seeking his presence. After all, it is in his presence that you find fullness of joy, and it is by entering his presence that you find rest. Prayer is simply stepping away from the busy world around you and taking God up on being his friend. God's presence is easiest to sense in the stillness of your mind and in the quiet moments of your day.

Even so, you will find that there is never more spiritual and mental static than when you try to pray. It sometimes seems as if the greater your efforts to stop and pray, the louder myriad

Do not be anxious about anything, but in everything by prayer and supplication with thanksgiving let your requests be made known to God. And the peace of God, which surpasses all understanding, will guard your hearts and your minds in Christ Jesus.

Philippians 4:6–7 ESV

concerns in your life shout for your attention. Julian of Norwich, a fourteenth-century hermit who devoted her life to God, hardly had myriad concerns drowning out her prayerful thoughts, but even she struggled with prayer. "Pray inwardly, even if you do not enjoy it," she advised. "It does good, though you feel nothing. Yes, even though you think you are doing nothing." If distractions aren't your problem, questions about the purpose of prayer may be. But prayer "does good," so don't lose heart. Start talking to God about both the distractions and your questions.

Many women have found that it helps to keep a prayer journal in which they record what they prayed about and how God answered those prayers. Be creative; write out your prayers if that helps you keep your focus. The writers of the book of Psalms often turned their prayers into songs, while other people have turned their prayers into poetry. Writing down your thoughts while you are praying can help you see that God is saying more to you than you think he is. Remember, too, that prayer doesn't need to be confined to a certain place and time in your day. As concerns pop up during the day, immediately pray a quick prayer to God—and don't forget to keep listening for his answers.

Think of your prayer time with God as you would think of having coffee with a friend—a time of intimate, one-on-one conversation. Talk to him about all your problems and ask for his help. God cares. Release your anxieties to him, and thank him for his blessings.

what's essential

 Prayer allows you to enter God's presence with the burdens of your life, give them all to him, and leave with the peace of God to carry you through the rest of the day. Friendship with God and clarity on his plans for your life develop in prayer.

DO approach prayer as a conversation that involves both talking and listening.

DO thank God that he is taking care of the problems and people you pray about.

DON'T allow distractions and your many daily responsibilities to rob you of your time with God.

DON'T leave your prayer time feeling anxious, but allow the peace of God to leave with you.

Pray for Others

When we pray for others, we enter side by side with Jesus into God's presence and get a glimpse of God's heart—his love for the world. Praying for others takes the focus off ourselves and allows us to see the people we care about from God's perspective.

The disciples asked Jesus to teach them to pray. In response, he taught them a simple outline for prayer, often called the Lord's Prayer. In it, he offered examples of the things they should talk about in their conversations with God: that God's name would be respected and revered, that his kingdom would continue to change lives, that daily needs would be met, that God would forgive his people and they would forgive others, and that he would protect his people from evil.

After that Jesus went on to tell the story of a friend who went to a neighbor at midnight to ask for food for an unexpected visitor. The neighbor didn't want to help at first; he said, "Don't bother me. The door is already locked, and my children are with me in bed. I can't get up and give you

Suppose one of you has a friend, and he goes to him at midnight and says, "Friend, lend me three loaves of bread, because a friend of mine on a journey has come to me, and I have nothing to set before him."

Luke 11:5–6 NIV

Jesus spent so much time in prayer because He knew that the time He spent talking with God about people did more for people than the time He spent talking with people about God.

P. T. Forsyth

anything" (Luke 11:7 NIV). But the friend wouldn't go away. According to the customs of the land, the need of any visitor was greater even than the need of the one providing hospitality. Sending a traveler away hungry was simply not done. So the one banging on the door shamelessly persisted, even to the point of being rude. The neighbor, seeing he had no chance of getting back to sleep until he helped, finally gave in and took bread to his friend so he could feed his guest and honor his responsibility to provide for his visitor.

The criterion for our intercessory prayer is not our earnestness, nor our faithfulness, nor even our faith in God, but simply God Himself . . . He asks us to present these requests to Him that He may show His gracious hand.
—Charles H. Troutman

It would be nice if those "visiting" you simply needed a few loaves of bread. Instead, you are more likely to have a friend who is struggling with depression or facing sickness or whose marriage is failing. Maybe she is struggling with substance abuse or has a close family member who is. Perhaps she just lost her job, had a terrible fight with her husband, or received yet another call from the school about her child's behavior. Whatever the situation, she doesn't know what to do—and she's turning to you, hoping that with you she'll find an answer, a reason to hope, or at the very least, a listening ear.

Thankfully, you are not alone in providing for your friend's needs. God can help. The point of Jesus' parable is to show you

interesting to note

In a 2007 analysis of seventeen major scientific studies on the effects of prayer on healing, an Arizona State researcher concluded that prayers offered on behalf of medical and psychiatric patients yielded positive results, countering the conclusions of a single, controversial, 2006 study.

I looked for someone to defend the city and to protect it from my anger, as well as to stop me from destroying it. But I found no one.

Ezekiel 22:30 CEV

that you can persist in asking God to meet your friend's need. Take your concerns to him regardless of the timing or the circumstances. Go to God even when it is inconvenient and continue banging on God's door until there is an answer. Enter his presence with a request on behalf of your friend with even more boldness than if you were asking for something for yourself.

If something is troubling you, pray about it. God may take care of the situation himself, he may give you the wisdom to resolve the problem, or he may bring someone into your life who holds the key to helping you figure out what to do. If your friend is in a troubling situation, God wants you to go to him in prayer about that as well. In showing your love and compassion for your friend, you're giving God an opportunity to show his love and compassion for her through you.

God never asks his people to shoulder their burdens alone. He wants you to come to him with your every concern, whether it's for yourself, your loved ones, your friends, or even strangers. Your prayers are never wasted. God always hears, always answers, and always provides. Keep at it! He'll never turn you away.

You can do many things to help those you care about, but the best thing you can do is pray for them. Trust God to give you or someone else the answers those people need to give them peace and help solve their problems.

what's essential

 Praying for others, which is known as intercessory prayer, allows you to grasp the depth of God's love and compassion for them—and maybe even his answers to whatever difficult situations they're experiencing.

DO be persistent in praying for the needs of the people you care about.

DO be open to the Holy Spirit to show you how to pray for others.

DON'T let the deteriorating circumstances in a friend's life discourage you from continuing to pray for her.

DON'T forget that God does not want or expect you to take on a friend's burdens without his help.

Listen for God to Answer

Prayer is communication with God—and that means much more than talking. Prayer is a way not only for God to empower you with divine wisdom and understanding but also for you to receive guidance and specific instruction for the circumstances of your life.

You've probably heard one of your friends say it—or maybe you've said it yourself: "I wish God would just come right out and tell me what he wants me to do!" What this means is that your friend or you want God to speak in an audible voice and make his desires clearly known. Obedience is the easy part; figuring out what he wants is the real challenge.

God could, of course, speak to you audibly if he wanted to. At times his voice thundered from the heavens as he spoke to Old Testament prophets. When the Holy Spirit came to earth after Jesus returned to heaven, the means God used to speak to his people changed dramatically. The Spirit became God's internal voice in the lives of his followers. The Bible speaks of the Spirit as not just being *with* them but as also living *in* them (John 14:17). This was an extraordinary change; God's people no longer had to rely on religious leaders—who in Jesus' day were hypocrites, according to Jesus himself—to hear God's voice. They could suddenly "hear" his voice internally.

 When I'm praying, when I'm truly praying, I'm not thinking, I'm not speaking, I'm shutting up, so perhaps if God has something to say I can hear it.
—Madeleine L'Engle

Listening for his voice, however, is only the beginning. You need to distinguish God's voice from your own thoughts and opinions. One of the best ways to do that is to compare what God is telling you with what is written in the Bible, because his guidance will always line up with what the Bible teaches. And that requires knowing what the Bible says. As you read the Bible, its teachings become not only more familiar but also more comprehensible. Teachings you didn't quite understand at first will begin to make more sense. Then, when you believe God is speaking to you, the whole experience won't seem so foreign. You'll be able to understand what he's asking of you, because it makes sense in the context of your Bible reading.

You also need to train yourself to respond to what God says. The more often you obey his voice, the more sensitive you will become to his voice. By contrast, the more you disregard it, the less distinguishable that voice will become. The temptation for many women is to become overly concerned about whether they

Were not our hearts burning within us while he talked with us on the road and opened the Scriptures to us?

Luke 24:32 NIV

can even *hear* God's voice in the clamor of their day, much less compare it with the Bible and then obey it. Remember: God is gracious and merciful. He'll help you silence the noise in your life and regain your composure. Maintaining that composure is like keeping your ear pressed against the door of heaven—the more attentive and obedient you are, the more likely it is that you will hear clearly.

What about those decisions you face that are not addressed by Scripture? It's not as if there are clear directives for all the details of your life. Is this the job God has for you, or should you look elsewhere? Is this Mr. Right, or should you wait for someone else? Is this the church God wants you to attend, or is it the one down the street? These aren't necessarily clear-cut, right-or-wrong decisions. In those situations you need specific answers—a yes or a no.

Those answers will come more easily as you spend time in prayer and Bible reading, because you will learn to recognize God's peace more readily. His peace means it's a yes; your uneasiness means it's a no.

Be patient. Listen for his voice. You'll no longer have to wish that God would come right out and tell you what he wants you to do; you'll already know, deep down inside.

God is interested in every aspect of your life. Go to him and ask his advice. Your assurance of his loving concern about the details of your life is more important than the details themselves. Focus on the relationship, and trust him with the decisions you have to make.

what's essential

 Learning to hear God's voice—and responding to it— is an essential aspect of your relationship with him. As you cultivate the ability to identify his voice, you'll be in a position to receive his wisdom, direction, and guidance for your life.

DO learn to distinguish between God's voice and your own thoughts.

DO spend time reading the Bible so you'll know if what you're hearing lines up with its teachings.

DON'T allow the noise in your life to drown out the voice of God.

DON'T become so worried about hearing God correctly that you forget how gracious he is.

Live by Praise and Gratitude

Praising God—expressing how awesome he is—is closely related to expressing gratitude to him. When you praise God for how wonderful he is, you can't help but feel grateful. And when you experience gratitude for something he has done in your life, you can't help but praise him.

Many women keep a gratitude journal, a notebook where they record all the things for which they're grateful. Some days, the entries may include the seemingly routine: gratitude for nice weather, a good day at work, a functioning washing machine. Other days, the notations are much more dramatic: gratitude for a negative mammogram screening, protection from a potentially deadly car crash, an unexpected check that will keep the lights on for another month. Most of these women understand well who deserves their gratitude, and their journals reflect that, with expressions like "Praise God!" punctuating many of the pages.

Take a moment to look around you and inventory all the things you have to be grateful for.

Material blessings are easy to recognize—a roof over your head, practical and maybe even comfortable furniture, your own car or access to public transportation, food in the pantry and the refrigerator. And there are the living blessings—people whom you love and who love you in return, good neighbors, a decent boss, a faithful dog that makes you feel as if you're the most wonderful person on earth. There's so much more to be grateful for that you hardly know where to start, and you certainly don't know when to stop. But you do know that all these good things didn't just materialize out of thin air. They're gifts from God, and your gratitude for them leads you straight into praising God.

 God is in control, and therefore in everything I can give thanks, not because of the situation, but because of the One who directs and rules over it.
—Kay Arthur

That's the beauty of gratitude. The more you express your gratefulness to God, the more grateful you become. Your one gratitude journal turns into multiple gratitude journals in no time. And praise? Well, that takes on a new dimension. Where you once thought of praise as something you included in your prayers, now you realize that your praise of God may erupt into a song or a dance or a way of skipping around the house that you don't even have a name for. Suddenly you're flinging your arms up toward heaven, even though that's something you never felt comfortable doing before. But who cares? You're praising God with sheer abandon and total delight.

interesting to note

Research funded by the John Templeton Foundation determined that while nonreligious people could feel grateful, people who regularly pray, attend religious services, and read religious material were more likely to be grateful than those who did not.

Rejoice in the Lord always. Again I will say, rejoice!

Philippians 4:4 NKJV

Praise and gratitude unlock the potential in life by revealing to you all that you have right now and offering hope for all that could be yours in the future. And that in turn releases a generosity of spirit in your life. Your arms not only stretch up toward heaven, but they also stretch out toward others, welcoming them into your life and extending to them all that God has to give through you. How can you not want to show others the abundance that could be theirs? Of course you want to! You want to grab your best friend and tell her, "Guess what God did for me? He's awesome! I can't stop thanking him!" And then you pull her into this amazing sphere where praise and gratitude prevail.

Will you always feel like praising God? Of course not. And that's okay. That's the way God's people are, and he understands that. Even David, who wrote beautiful songs of praise in the book of Psalms, also expressed his frustration with God in the same book—sometimes even in the same song! More often than not, however, he ended up praising God in the midst of the many trials he faced. It is often in moments of trial that God has a way of reminding his people of just how much they have to be grateful for. A return to praise is almost inevitable. Make gratitude a habit by remembering all that God has given you, and praise is sure to follow.

Start your own gratitude journal, remembering to whom it's written. Express your gratefulness to God, and be sure to include the words of praise that come to your mind as you list the things you're thankful for. When you're discouraged, go back and read what you've written.

what's essential

Praise and gratitude acknowledge that God is above any circumstance you may face. Your expressions of praise and gratitude honor God and let him know how thankful you are not only for what he has done for you but also for the simple fact that he *is*.

DO read the Psalms and let David teach you how to praise God in the midst of adversity.

DO sprinkle your daily conversations with expressions of gratitude.

DON'T allow inhibitions to keep you from letting praise erupt into singing, dancing, or laughing.

DON'T let those times when you feel unable to praise God prevent you from returning to an attitude of praise as soon as possible.

Hope

The eyes of the LORD are on those
who fear him, on those whose
hope is in his unfailing love,
to deliver them from death
and keep them alive in fam-
ine. We wait in hope for the
LORD; he is our help and our
shield. In him our hearts rejoice, for we trust in his holy
name. May your unfailing
love rest upon us, O LORD,
even as we put our hope in
you.
　　　　Psalm 33:18–22 NIV

Hope is the feeling you have that
the feeling you have isn't permanent.
　　　　Jean Kerr

Hope begins in the dark, the stubborn hope
that if you just show up and try to do the right
thing, the dawn will come.
　　　　Anne Lamott

Know Your Part in God's Family

When you came into a relationship with God, you became a part of his family—the church. There's a special place for you in that family, a role that is yours alone to fill. This may be just the time for you to take your rightful place in the family of God and begin to fill that role.

I n the earliest days of Christianity, the idea of a church building was unknown; Christians gathered in homes to study the Scriptures, to worship God together, and, on a really special day, to hear someone read the latest letter from a distant Christian leader. Today, the word *church* has become synonymous with two things: the building Christians meet in and the meetings themselves. People talk about "going to church," but that's simply a function and limitation of language. In reality, the church is much larger than any building or meeting on earth could possibly accommodate.

Seeing the church as the family of God is helpful on many levels. The Bible even uses family terms to describe how you join the church—by

Let's see how inventive we can be in encouraging love and helping out, not avoiding worshiping together as some do but spurring each other on, especially as we see the big Day approaching.
Hebrews 10:24–25 MSG

Church isn't where you meet. Church isn't a building. Church is what you do. Church is who you are. Church is the human outworking of the person of Jesus Christ. Let's not go to church; let's be the church.
Bridget Willard

being "born again" or adopted into it. As with your earthly family, when you reach a certain age you can choose not to attend family gatherings, but that doesn't change your status as a family member. You have a connection that transcends circumstances, preferences, personality types—even time and space.

 The faithful . . . ought to have an ever-clearer consciousness not only of belonging to the Church, but of being the Church.
—Pope John Paul II

But here's the rub: you don't get to choose your relatives in God's family. If they're related to God, they're related to you, like it or not. And the usual family dynamics often come into play. Older relatives—in the case of the church, those who have known God a bit longer than the rest—have certain ideas about how things should be done, sometimes based on genuine wisdom and sometimes on long-standing personal preference. But along come the rowdy, energetic young people, who intend to inject a different kind of life into these family get-togethers. In the midst of that, siblings try to hide their underlying rivalry but rarely succeed. And in any gathering of God's family, you're likely to find the crazy uncle whom everyone tolerates with varying degrees of amusement.

You can avoid the dynamics of family life by avoiding family gatherings, but doing so won't change the fact that you have a special place in that family, whether it's your earthly family or God's family. You are someone's sister, daughter, aunt, cousin, niece, granddaughter, or maybe even mother or grandmother.

Your absence creates a void in the family that no one else can fill. A sister who doesn't seem to miss you at all secretly *does*; she may not show it, but your presence could be a source of great comfort to her. A niece who acts much too cool for the likes of you may silently—and desperately—wish that you would show up, because you're the one person who loves her in spite of herself. You have a role in the family, and you have a lot to give in fulfilling that role.

You also have a lot to receive, especially when it comes to the family of God. Getting together with other family members can help you get to know God better and follow him more closely. Seeing how other Christians fulfill their roles in the family helps you understand your own role better. In its purest form, the family of God is a safe place where you are nurtured and prepared to take on the challenges of everyday life. Even in its dysfunctional form, God's family serves a distinct purpose as a place where you learn to have love and compassion for people you would not choose to have a relationship with were they not family members.

By taking your place in God's family, assuming the role you were meant to fulfill, and joining in the family gatherings, you'll realize that following

interesting to note

In a second-century letter, a pagan described the early church in this way: "They obey the prescribed laws, and at the same time, they surpass the laws by their lives . . . They are poor, yet they make many rich. They possess few things; yet, they abound in all . . . And those who hate them are unable to give any reason for their hatred."

You are no longer strangers and aliens, but you are fellow citizens with the saints and members of the household of God, built on the foundation of the apostles and prophets, Christ Jesus himself being the cornerstone.
Ephesians 2:19–20 ESV

God isn't about *going* to church—it's about *being* the church, a member of his family.

Jesus said people would recognize his followers by the love they had for one another (John 13:35). Genuine, lasting love is forged in the difficulties that all relationships face—including those in God's family. Make it a point to love his family, no matter how difficult that may sometimes be.

what's essential

 Lutheran pastor Richard Kuehn once said, "The purpose of church is that we might learn to love unconditionally those we wouldn't normally like." By choosing to participate in God's family, you are learning one of life's essentials—how to love as God loves.

DO realize that as a follower of God, you are already a member of his family.

DO recognize that God has given you a special role to fulfill.

DON'T allow family problems to keep you from participating in gatherings of God's family.

DON'T forget that your absence leaves a void that no one else can fill.

Plan Your Getaways with God

What woman doesn't love a getaway— a time to escape the hustle and bustle of daily routines and find some peace and quiet? For many women, such a notion is a fantasy, but it doesn't have to be. You can enjoy brief, refreshing getaways with God every day.

Are you tired? Worn out? Burned out on religion? Come to me. Get away with me and you'll recover your life. I'll show you how to take a real rest.

Matthew 11:28 MSG

Fifty years ago, experts predicted that emerging technologies would so streamline Americans' lives that one of the results would be a life of leisure—or at least, *more* leisure. The average workweek would be reduced to thirty-two hours, and the stay-at-home wives and mothers who were the norm at that time would have more time to pursue hobbies and other enjoyable activities.

The experts were wrong. New technology has instead complicated people's lives by making it possible to work twenty-four/seven—if their bodies would only let them. It has also created a fast-paced lifestyle that for many people is a reality and for many others a mind-set, an illusion that their lives have to be in constant motion when in fact they don't.

When I find myself racing around, trying to fill a day with mindless tasks or petty entertainment, this is usually the time that God whispers to my heart to draw away with Him and to silence my heart as He wishes to speak.

Katherine Walden

In the midst of this never-ending activity, God says, "Come away with me and rest awhile." What an enticing invitation! *Rest.* What a beautiful word! *If only I could,* you think. *If only I could get away and really rest.* Well, God extends that invitation while anticipating your every objection: You don't have the time. There's too much to do. You can't afford a retreat. If you're a mother, you can't get a babysitter. His response? "Come away with me and rest awhile."

 Why is it so important that you are with God and God alone on the mountain top? It's important because it's the place in which you can listen to the voice of the One who calls you the beloved.
—Henri J. M. Nouwen

Take a deep breath. Relax your shoulders. Think of ways you can make this happen. Since God is the one inviting you, it must be possible, right? Ask for his help. He's beckoning you to join him in a time of restoration and rejuvenation. He didn't set a mandatory, minimum time restriction. He didn't say you had to go on an official retreat. And he didn't utter a word about spending money. He wants you to see this as a time when you can be alone with him, draw on his strength, and return to your regular life with newfound energy and a renewed perspective.

All you need is a few minutes and a willingness to shut the world out and turn your heart and thoughts toward God. Having your Bible close is helpful, but if it isn't nearby, you can still enjoy these quiet moments with God. A notebook is useful, too, especially if writing helps you focus. More important than making sure you have all the right equipment with you, however, is spending this time with God.

The biggest challenge is finding the time and place for your getaway. Some women get up earlier than they need to in order to spend undistracted time with God. Others find that staying up later affords them this opportunity. If neither situation works for you, think outside the home. Be creative. As you're driving home from work, be on the lookout for a safe spot. When you see one, pull over to pray, read your Bible, or journal, even if it means staying in your car. Or go for a walk and pray as you take each step. Sit on a park bench and just *be* with God. Release the pressure to perform and to be productive. Rest in God's presence.

Appreciate your time alone with God for the grace-filled interlude that it is. Think of every wonderful word you can that describes what your soul needs—*replenishment, renewal, peace, tranquillity*—and approach your time with God with those words in mind. This is what he wants you to have—a daily oasis that transforms the fatigue, tensions, and stresses of life into the rest and refreshment you need.

interesting to note

Susanna Wesley, mother of historic church leaders John and Charles Wesley, gave birth to nineteen children, ten of whom survived. Despite all the pregnancies and childrearing, she found a way to have a quiet time. She pulled her apron over her head—and her children knew to leave her alone.

Very early in the morning, while it was still dark, Jesus got up, left the house and went off to a solitary place, where he prayed.

Mark 1:35 NIV

It's to your advantage to spend time with God each day. If you're a creature of habit, establish a regular time and place that is reserved exclusively for him. If you're a free spirit, be inventive in deciding how you will meet with God on any given day.

what's essential

 Setting aside time to spend with God is essential, especially in a society that seldom sleeps. Without putting some intentional effort into it, you're likely to let the many details of your life crowd out your time with God. Make sure you place a high priority on that time.

DO make your time with God so pleasant that you wouldn't think of missing it.

DO be creative when it comes to deciding how you'll spend your time with God.

DON'T allow a fast-paced culture to deprive you of your need for rest and refreshment.

DON'T worry about all the errands and chores you think you should be taking care of.

Live to Always Please God

Most women have a deep desire to please other people. When they come into relationship with God, that desire often expands to include the need to please God. The willingness is already there; what they may need is a clearer understanding of how effortless it can be to truly please God.

Women have a knack for making their lives harder than they need to be. Most women feel they should be doing more, more, more, all the time. It's likely that you place pressure on yourself to accomplish a great deal in a single day. And much of what you accomplish is done in an effort to please someone else. If you're not careful, you can transfer that pressure to perform to your relationship with God and convince yourself that you must fulfill a host of demands that he never actually placed on you.

What does it take to please God? Surprisingly little. In fact, if you think of your life as a gift from him and to him, you're well on your way toward pleasing him. What that means in practical terms

We ask God to give you complete knowledge of his will and to give you spiritual wisdom and understanding. Then the way you live will always honor and please the Lord, and your lives will produce every kind of good fruit. All the while, you will grow as you learn to know God better and better.

Colossians 1:9–10 NLT

The serene, silent beauty of a holy life is the most powerful influence in the world, next to the might of the Spirit of God.

Blaise Pascal

85

is this: in gratitude for the life he has given you, you present your life back to him as an offering, a gift. In essence, you say, "Here I am, God. Do with me what you will." You place your life in his hands and express your willingness to please him, trusting that he will always have your best interests at heart.

It is not a difficult matter to learn what it means to delight ourselves in the Lord. It is to live so as to please Him, to honor everything we find in His Word, to do everything the way He would like to have it done, and for Him.
—S. Maxwell Coder

To assure you that you are on the right track, the Bible offers several insights into some specific things you can do to please God. Jesus addressed this very subject once when the religious scholars of his day tried to trip him up by asking him which of the commandments was the greatest. It's hard to know what answer they expected, but it certainly wasn't the one he gave. He said, "'Love the Lord your God with all your passion and prayer and intelligence.' This is the most important, the first on any list. But there is a second to set alongside it: 'Love others as well as you love yourself'" (Matthew 22:37–39 MSG).

Jesus stated it clearly. You please God by loving him and loving other people. He repeated the second part of that answer when he was talking to his closest followers. There, he emphasized the need for them to love other followers of God: "I am giving you a new commandment: Love each other. Just as I have loved you, you should love each other" (John 13:34 NLT).

As simple as that sounds, living it out is another matter. In order to please God, your love for other people has to be genuine. If you're not careful, you can overthink this—another way women complicate their lives—and end up worrying if your love is real. God has the answer for that problem; ask him to give you his love for other people as you're in the process of learning how God's love is activated in your life.

God is looking for women who are willing to walk with him and learn to see other people as he sees them, just as Jesus did when he was on earth. Having God's perspective helps you to know how to love others. He's looking for women who long to know him better, to love him with all their hearts, and to follow him completely. If you fit that description, begin to see yourself as he sees you—as a woman full of promise and of unique importance to him.

And your efforts to please people? They take a backseat to pleasing God. The apostle Paul said this: "I am not trying to please people. I want to please God. Do you think I am trying to please people? If I were doing that, I would not be a servant of Christ" (Galatians 1:10 CEV). It's much more rewarding to be a servant of Christ than to be a people-pleaser.

Pleasing God means caring about what he cares about and living accordingly. When your desire to please God becomes a state of being within you, you will no longer worry about whether your life is pleasing to him; you can rest assured that it will be.

what's essential

 Pleasing God involves seeing things as he sees them.

DO please God by loving him with all your heart, mind, and spirit.

DO learn to see other people from God's perspective.

DON'T try to please people in your own strength when you could love them with God's love.

DON'T try to meet demands that God never placed on you in the first place.

Keep God Near

Between a deep desire for meaningful relationship and a deep need for love and respect, many women whose hearts are open to spiritual truth eagerly embrace the God of the Bible. So why would any woman need to be told to "draw near to God"?

Telling a woman to draw near to God seems almost like telling her to breathe. When women come into a relationship with God, drawing near to him practically becomes second nature, at least at first. As life settles back into an everyday routine marked by multitasking and numerous responsibilities, now and then a gentle reminder to stay close to God may be needed. But for the most part, women don't often need those reminders; the comfort they find in God has a magnetic pull on their lives.

There is one factor, however, that causes some women to keep God at arm's length: shame. Women are especially vulnerable to feelings of shame, often connected to situations they had little or no control over, situations such as incest, rape, and

> Draw near to God and He will draw near to you.
>
> **James 4:8** NKJV

> It is important that we get still to wait on God. And it is best that we get alone, preferably with our Bible outspread before us. Then if we will we may draw near to God and begin to hear Him speak to us in our hearts.
>
> A. W. Tozer

physical abuse. Situations that they *did* have control over—promiscuity, addiction, abortion, and others—produce so much guilt that some women become convinced that God wants nothing to do with them. Other women *want* to respond to God's love but feel so unworthy that they cannot even accept the notion of God's love, much less the love itself. Still others feel that they have to get their act together before they can approach God; they're so ashamed of their shame that they want to get rid of it and only *then* turn to God.

In tribulation immediately draw near to God with confidence, and you will receive strength, enlightenment, and instruction.
—Saint John of the Cross

One result of all these responses to shame is spiritual paralysis. How can you draw near to God when you're so stuck that you can't move? Here's where more good news about God comes into play. If you've never asked God for his forgiveness, you'll be relieved to know that his forgiveness covers your reluctance to turn to him, your feelings of shame, and any responsibility you may have had in the situations that caused your shame. His love and compassion are more powerful than the shame you feel. He freely bestows his grace—his divine approval—on you. And he promises that when you move closer to him, he will move closer to you.

In reality, God made the first move in your direction long ago. Jesus' ministry demonstrated God's willingness to take the first step in breaking the barrier between heaven and earth. The kingdom of God, he said, was "at hand" (Matthew 3:2 NKJV)—all around you and well within your reach. In the book of Acts, the kingdom of God came even nearer when the Spirit of God began to live inside the followers of God. If all that's true— and it is—then what does it mean to "draw near" to God? And why should you have to do it at all?

Throughout the Bible, God searched for people who would intentionally respond to the many offers of forgiveness, grace, mercy, reward, and renewal that he extended to them. One way you demonstrate your intention to accept those offers and follow him is by coming into close communication with him through prayer, reading the Bible to get to know him and what he wants you to do, and following the direction of the Holy Spirit— in essence, drawing near to him. When you do, you can have the confidence of knowing that he is closer than ever.

Allow God to shatter the barrier of shame that may be separating you from him. Don't wait until you feel as if you have it all together—no woman ever has it all together, by the way, even when shame isn't a factor—or when you feel worthy of his love. Draw near to him now. Turn your heart toward him

interesting to note

Ministries to women who suffer from feelings of shame are right at your fingertips. A quick Internet search for terms like *women, shame, and abortion,* for example, will yield dozens of results, including ministries that offer help lines and a wealth of other resources.

We have a great high priest who is in charge of God's house. So let's come near God with pure hearts and a confidence that comes from having faith.

Hebrews 10:21–22 CEV

and discover just how worthy he thinks you are. Soon enough, drawing near to him will become second nature to you as well.

Whenever memories of shameful situations arise, take that as a positive sign—a reminder that it's time to turn to God in gratitude for transforming your life with his offer of grace, forgiveness, and compassion.

what's essential

 Drawing near to God is an act of faith as much as it is a practice. You may not always feel God's presence, but remember this: the kingdom of God is all around you, and his Spirit lives inside you. Even if you can't sense his presence, he is there.

DO act on God's promise that he will move closer to you when you draw near to him.

DO allow God to remove any barriers that may be keeping you from confidently approaching him.

DON'T let shame or guilt keep you from enjoying the presence of God.

DON'T ever think that you are unworthy of God's love, compassion, and forgiveness.

Understand the Fear of the Lord

The Bible says that the beginning of wisdom is the fear of God. The fear of God? For women who have experienced the amazing love and forgiveness of God, the thought of fearing him is a foreign one. But once you understand that fear, you'll clearly see the connection.

I f you are in right relationship with God—if you are living in a way that is pleasing to him—you need never be afraid of God. If you have an accurate understanding of who he is, however, then you already have a working definition of the fear of the Lord: a reverence and awe for a holy God who, as author Jim Elliff puts it, is "not to be trifled with." He has the power to create and destroy, to reward and punish, to bless and curse. Those who follow and obey him need only be concerned about his power to create, reward, and bless, while never forgetting the counterparts to those actions.

A verse in the New Testament book of Hebrews makes it clear that you have no reason to, in a sense, fear the fear of God: "Since we are receiving a kingdom which cannot be shaken, let us have grace, by

The fear of the LORD is the beginning of wisdom; a good understanding have all those who do His commandments. His praise endures forever.

Psalm 111:10 NKJV

To fear God means that my life is structured by a sense of awe, worship, and obedience that flows out of recognizing Him and His glory . . . The fear of God is meant to be the central organizing force in my life.

Paul David Tripp

which we may serve God acceptably with reverence and godly fear" (12:28 NKJV). God gives you the grace to serve him with reverence and a godly fear in his kingdom, which cannot be destroyed.

 All the graces of Christianity always go together . . . where there is love, there is also trust; and where there is a holy trust in God; there is love to God; and where there is a gracious hope, there also is a holy fear of God.
—Jonathan Edwards

The fear of God works to your advantage in any number of ways. Here are a few Bible verses that place the fear of God in a positive light for those who have a healthy relationship with him. Those who fear the Lord will

- lack nothing (Psalm 34:9);

- receive God's compassion (Psalm 103:13);

- find favor with God (Psalm 147:11);

- have good things stored up for them (Psalm 31:19);

- find security (Proverbs 14:26);

- be kept safe (Proverbs 19:23);

- receive wealth, honor, and life (Proverbs 22:4).

Still, you may be wondering how this fear is the first step in acquiring wisdom. Look at it this way: you need to understand who God is, how he is working in the world today, and what his relationship is to people on earth before you can comprehend the depths of his wisdom. When you do understand who God is (the holy Creator of the universe and all that is in it), how he is working in the world today (empowering his people to transform the earth by establishing kingdom principles there), and what his relationship is to people on earth (he is the supreme authority over everyone), you begin to experience the fear of the Lord. And then you can start to comprehend his wisdom.

That kind of fear—the fear that leads to wisdom—is the kind known as *holy fear*. It's not that far removed from the fear you may have known as a young girl. If your father was a loving disciplinarian, you probably caught a glimpse of the kind of fear the Bible says God's followers should have. A loving father wouldn't make you afraid of him, but as a disciplinarian, he would make you aware of the consequences of your disobedience. From that you would glean various bits of wisdom, such as the value of living in accordance with certain moral and ethical guidelines. That's the kind of wisdom the fear of the Lord teaches you as well.

Yes, God is awesome and mighty. Yes, he should be approached with reverence and holy fear. Yes, he is not one to be trifled with. But he is also the one who loves you, rewards you, and blesses you with every good thing. And any fear you experience is transformed into perfect love, as the apostle John wrote: "There

interesting to note

Though people are most likely to acquire an understanding of the fear of the Lord all on their own, it's also something that can be taught, according to Psalm 34:11: "Come, O children, listen to me; I will teach you the fear of the LORD" (ESV).

Charm is deceptive, and beauty is fleeting; but a woman who fears the LORD is to be praised.
Proverbs 31:30 NIV

is no fear in love, but perfect love casts out fear. For fear has to do with punishment, and whoeer fears has not been perfected in love" (1 John 4:18 ESV).

As you come across references to the fear of the Lord in your Bible reading, pay attention to the distinction between the kind of fear his followers have and that which his enemies have—along with the rewards and punishments that each group faces.

what's essential

 As long as you are in right relationship with God, you will never have a reason to be afraid of him. Having a holy fear of him, however, reflects your understanding that a loving and compassionate God is still the powerful Creator who deserves your awe and reverence.

DO acquire a healthy comprehension of what the fear of the Lord is—and what it is not.

DO remember all the benefits that accompany the fear of the Lord.

DON'T ever be afraid of approaching the God who loves you.

DON'T misinterpret the fear of the Lord as a negative understanding of who God is.

God's Presence

Let the godly rejoice. Let them be glad in God's presence. Let them be filled with joy. Sing praises to God and to his name! Sing loud praises to him who rides the clouds. His name is the LORD—rejoice in his presence! Father to the fatherless, defender of widows—this is God, whose dwelling is holy. God places the lonely in families; he sets the prisoners free and gives them joy.

Psalm 68:3–6 NLT

We all go through pain and sorrow, but the presence of God, like a warm, comforting blanket, can shield us and protect us and allow the deep inner joy to surface, even in the most devastating circumstances.

Barbara Johnson

God is everything. My focus must be on him, seeking to know him more completely and allowing him full possession of my life.

Mary Morrison Suggs

Do the Right Thing

Talk radio host Dr. Laura Schlessinger ends each show with this simple piece of advice: "Now, go do the right thing." Simple advice maybe, but not always easy to follow. Doing the right thing sometimes means doing the exact opposite of what you feel like doing.

Inspiring stories of people doing the right thing tend to show up in the last few minutes of the evening newscast. A waitress with an unemployed husband, a critically ill baby, and a mountain of medical bills finds an envelope containing thousands of dollars in cash and turns it in to her manager. An Amish community reaches out to the family of a man who took the lives of five Amish girls. A teenager risks his life and suffers serious injury saving two young girls from a pit bull attack.

Inspiring stories, to be sure. But every day, people face opportunities to make far less dramatic decisions to do the right thing. They won't make the evening news, but their actions reverberate through the culture nonetheless. Doing the right thing—acting in accordance with your God-given understanding of what is right—can have a ripple effect that you'll never see. God sees it, though, and he's not at all surprised at the far-reaching influence of your behavior. This is the way life was meant to work all along.

Think of times when you've done something you didn't want to do—but you did it anyway because it was the right thing to do. A sister-in-law treated you badly, but you still help her out when she gets in a jam. You brave the pouring rain to go back into a store to pay for an unpaid tube of toothpaste that got stuck in a grocery cart hinge. Or one night when you were dog tired and just wanted to chill, you instead drove across town to listen to a brokenhearted friend pour out her sorrow.

 Because it's possible to do, and you have the right to do it, doesn't mean it's the right thing to do.
—Laura Schlessinger

Those hypothetical scenarios may not mirror your life, but it's likely that you've faced similar situations. And while they are all examples of doing the right thing, they also present several pitfalls that women are especially vulnerable to, such as "making nice" and martyrdom. Both situations result when women do the right things for the wrong reasons. If you're helping your sister-in-law because that's what "good little girls" are supposed to do, that's making nice, and that stems from a set of misguided expectations and obligations. If you even hint to your friend that it was a sacrifice to visit her when you were so tired, that's

interesting to note

Families of the victims of the Unabomber, Ted Kaczynski, whose mail bombs killed three people and injured twenty-three, received compensation from an unexpected source: Ted's brother David, who said sharing a $1 million reward with them was simply the right thing to do.

martyrdom. Even though people still benefit from your actions, when you do the right thing with the wrong attitude, you're not acting in a way that's pleasing to God.

God wants you to live your life under the direction and guidance of the Holy Spirit, and he wants your actions to be a response to the Spirit's leading. Doing the right thing with the right attitude and under the guidance of the Spirit ensures that your motives are pure and accurately reflect the nature of God. That in turn builds Christlike character in you and keeps your relationship with God on solid footing. And there's no telling the effect your genuinely selfless actions have on the people around you. People are watching you, and most people—especially women—can sniff out artificial motives from a pretty decent distance. But they can also sense the real thing, and actions that spring from a loving and compassionate heart bear the aroma of authenticity.

Many decisions pose a right or wrong dilemma. The book of James bluntly addresses those situations: "If you know the right thing to do and don't do it, that, for you, is evil" (James 4:17 MSG). Sometimes, though, you face right or *right* dilemmas, when both choices seem to be the

> It is God's will that your honorable lives should silence those ignorant people who make foolish accusations against you.
>
> **1 Peter 2:15** NLT

correct one. And that's when you need to make sure the Spirit is guiding you.

The next time you catch yourself doing the right thing when you'd rather do something else, pay attention to your attitude. If your action resulted in joy or even amusement, you can be fairly certain that your motives were pure and pleasing to God.

what's essential

 Doing the right thing with the right attitude and the right motivation reflects well on the way you respond to the Spirit and helps build Christlike character in you.

DO make sure that your motives are pure when you do something you don't want to do.

DO understand that your right actions have implications you will probably never be aware of.

DON'T fall into the traps of martyrdom or making nice—the "good little girl" syndrome.

DON'T let a wrong attitude undermine the good things you do for others.

Trust in God's Purposes

You are an integral part of God's plan for humanity, and the quality of your life is directly connected to fulfilling the purpose God has for you. When you stay true to God's course—even though you won't know how all the steps along the way fit together—you'll discover that purpose.

If you believe that God is your Creator, then you have to believe that he created you for a purpose—because God created *everything* for a purpose. He placed you on earth at this time for any number of reasons, including events he wants you to witness or participate in, things he wants you to do, and wisdom he wants you to bring to certain situations. Before you were born, he knew what he had in mind for you. If you trust in the purposes that he has for you, and if you follow the guidance of the Holy Spirit, you can't help but have a fulfilling life.

To God, you are a work of art, a perfectly fine example of his craftsmanship. Ephesians 2:10 says this: "We are God's masterpiece. He has created us anew in Christ Jesus, so we can do the good things he planned for us long ago" (NLT). Those "good things" include both blessings and challenges, like relationships that bring you great joy even as they test your mettle. God's plans sometimes start out looking pretty rough, but they have a refining quality to them that smoothes out the edges of your life. God is right there the entire time, whether you sense his presence or not, guiding you through times of difficulty. If you trust him and learn from those trials, it's less likely that you'll have to experience them again— and if you do, you'll do a much better job of handling them. You can be confident that God will be there to see you through. The writer of the book of Hebrews assured the early Christians of God's steady presence by quoting several Old Testament verses in which God said, "I will never leave you nor forsake you" (13:5 NKJV). In fact, the word *never* loses a lot in the English translation; in the original, it carries the connotation of "never, never, never!"

Nothing matters more than knowing God's purposes for your life, and nothing can compensate for not knowing them.
—Rick Warren

Hold tight to promises like that and others, such as the promises God made that if you seek him, you will find him (Jeremiah 29:13) and if you draw near to him, he will draw near to you (James 4:8). As you draw closer to him, do so with the expectation that he will reveal to you a part of what your purpose is.

interesting to note

The seventeenth-century Westminster Shorter Catechism states that the chief purpose in life is "to glorify God, and to enjoy him for ever." The phrase "enjoy him for ever" is among the best-known—and best-loved—sentiments among all historical documents of the Christian Church.

Do not be ashamed of the testimony about our Lord, nor of me his prisoner, but share in suffering for the gospel by the power of God, who saved us and called us to a holy calling, not because of our works but because of his own purpose and grace.

2 Timothy 1:8–9 ESV

Sometimes, all it takes is to look at your circumstances from God's perspective. Look at where he has placed you, and ask him why you are where you are. Why are you living in the town you're in, doing the job you're doing? Maybe you're supposed to find your purpose right where you are—or maybe where you are will turn out to be a springboard to something different. Ask God to either give you peace about your situation or show you what you need to do to experience his peace.

Trust that God has your best interests at heart. Walk with the confidence of a woman who knows she has every reason to expect good things to come her way—because you do, since "every reason" stems from the promises of God. Consider those promises as you seek his purpose for your life. And don't forget to consider your talents and the things you're passionate about. Give everything you have to fulfilling God's purpose for your life.

Humorist Erma Bombeck once said: "When I stand before God at the end of my life, I would hope that I would not have a single bit of talent left and could say, 'I used everything you gave me.'" Couple that sentiment with the Spirit's guidance, and there's little doubt that you'll fulfill God's purpose for your life.

Seek God's purpose for your life by staying focused on him, following the guidance of the Holy Spirit, and paying attention to where God has placed you and the talents and skills he has given you. The rest will take care of itself.

what's essential

 God has a special purpose for your life, and you can trust that he has your best interests at heart in revealing your purpose and enabling you to fulfill it.

DO believe that you are God's masterpiece, created for a particular purpose.

DO pray to make sure that whatever task you have before you is part of God's purpose for you.

DON'T let your present circumstances discourage you from believing that God has good things in store for you.

DON'T forget that God has promised to "never, never, never!" leave you.

Keep Things Simple

Theology—literally, the study of God—can get complicated quickly. Theological study certainly has its place. But when it comes to living out your faith on a day-to-day basis, nothing beats a simple, childlike faith that believes God will do what he says he will do.

Simplicity has become something of a buzzword in the U.S. in recent years. People are making an intentional effort to simplify their lives by reducing the demands on their schedules, eliminating the clutter in their homes, and cutting back on the number of things that come into the house, from subscription magazines to electronic gadgets to an extra bag of chips.

Far fewer people, however, are aware of another kind of clutter that creates just as much stress but is much harder to recognize: mental clutter. You can't see it, you can't throw it away, and you can't give it away. People of God are vulnerable to a special brand of mental overload: theological clutter. This kind of clutter is especially easy to accumulate, because it has to do with God— and you can't ignore anything that has to do with

Something of true value does not become more valuable because it becomes complicated . . . Complications arise and fall away, but the simple action of God is eternal in the universe.

Donald Curtis

God, right? You understandably want to know everything there is to know about God, so you start to read faith-related books and study your Bible. So far so good. Studying to learn more about this journey of faith that you've embarked on is one of the best ways you can spend your time.

It is the sweet, simple things of life which are the real ones after all.
—Laura Ingalls Wilder

Theological study reaches the clutter threshold when it begins to interfere with your relationship with God. The centuries-old debate over how many angels could dance on the point of a needle became a symbol for time-wasting, useless theological arguments. Today, all you have to do is enter a religious question into an Internet search engine, and you'll discover the modern-day equivalent of time-wasting, useless arguments; page after page of arguments over what God *really* meant in any given biblical passage clutter the results and obscure those pages that might actually hold the answer to your question. In Jesus' time and even long before, religious leaders debated the finer points of theology and in the process added so many man-made rules to God's commandments that following those rules became impossible. There were too many, and the burden they placed on the people was just too much to bear.

Imagine the relief Jesus brought to the people with his message of love and freedom and acceptance. Those who caught the deeper meaning of his teachings understood that he was preaching a

I didn't try to impress you with polished speeches and the latest philosophy. I deliberately kept it plain and simple: first Jesus and who he is; then Jesus and what he did.

1 Corinthians 2:1–2 MSG

message of simple faith. This was most apparent one day when a group of women brought their children to him for a blessing. His disciples saw the children as a bother. But Jesus used that occasion to teach his disciples yet another lesson about the kingdom of God: "I tell you the truth, anyone who will not receive the kingdom of God like a little child will never enter it" (Luke 18:17 NIV). The mothers certainly understood what he meant, because they knew how trusting their children could be. God wanted followers who trusted him the way little children trust their parents.

The essential habits of your life with God should exhibit that same childlike trust and simplicity. Believe that God will do what he says he will do. Follow Jesus' example. Tell the truth. Love God. Love other people. Don't take what isn't yours. Don't even *want* what isn't yours. Don't do anything hurtful. Watch your tongue. Treat people with respect. Spend time with God. Pray. Be grateful. Give.

One of the most familiar sayings of Henry David Thoreau bears repeating here: "Our life is frittered away by detail. Simplify, simplify, simplify!" He wasn't referring to faith, but his words apply all the same. Don't fritter your life away by complicating your life with God. Simplify, simplify, simplify!

Keep your faith simple by focusing on what matters most: pleasing God by living your life according to the very clear guidelines he gave in the Bible and the personal leading of the Holy Spirit in your own life.

what's essential

 It's all too easy to complicate your relationship with God with theological arguments and requirements for living that do not come from God. Having a childlike faith—a trusting relationship with God—is what's essential.

DO simplify your life with God by focusing on the behavior and character traits that are most pleasing to him.

DO study the Bible and read faith-related books, keeping that theological-clutter threshold in mind.

DON'T waste your time on theological arguments that have no bearing on your relationship with God.

DON'T complicate your faith life by mixing man-made rules with the guidelines God gave for right living.

Attempt Big Things for God

Simple faith can lead to amazing things. A single act of kindness can have a ripple effect that has an impact on countless people. It could even lead to something much bigger, like a project that fights poverty or injustice and in the process changes lives.

God can do anything, you know—far more than you could ever imagine or guess or request in your wildest dreams! He does it not by pushing us around but by working within us, his Spirit deeply and gently within us.

Ephesians 3:20 MSG

The evening news often includes stories that show the immense power of simple actions. A young girl who came across a man sleeping in the streets began a campaign to collect blankets for the homeless. Students from a local grade school traded their candy bags on Halloween for coin boxes to raise money to help hungry families. A couple on a mission trip to Africa adopted an orphanage to support. A family sponsored a child in India. A woman concerned about battered mothers opened a safe house for them and their children. Another opened a home for pregnant teenagers, and soon such homes were in five different cities. Yet another started a nonprofit that teaches teens the relationship skills they need to remain abstinent until marriage, preventing such

I do not pray for a lighter load, but for a stronger back.

Phillips Brooks

pregnancies in the first place. A missionary started a jewelry-making company whose proceeds help rescue women and children from prostitution. A simple idea in the hands of God can snowball into something that changes the face of a community.

It's understandable to feel overwhelmed when you look at the enormous problems in the world; you feel powerless against the magnitude of the need. Yet all the preceding stories started with individuals who discovered a need and sensed that God was calling them to do something about it. As they have shown, the first step toward meeting a need is as simple as asking, "What can I do to help?"

 If we are not thinking, hoping, or asking for anything, we are cheating ourselves. We need to think big thoughts, hope for big things, and ask for big things.
—Joyce Meyer

God is looking for ordinary people to do extraordinary things for him to address the problems the world faces today. You may be the one in a million who donates to a certain cause, someone who spearheads a movement, or someone who prays behind the scene to welcome God's presence into a specific dilemma. God may want you to be a small part of an organization or the founder of one. Or he might just want you to start a group that will pray about it at your church and to follow his lead from there. The idea is to take it one small, God-guided step at a time. As the proverb goes, a journey of a thousand miles still begins with one footstep.

God is bigger than any of earth's problems, and throughout history his people have accomplished big things to solve those problems. In 1852 Harriet Beecher Stowe took the gift God had given her—writing—and used it to expose the brutality and injustice of slave life in the book *Uncle Tom's Cabin,* helping to set into motion the events that led to the abolition of slavery. Despite being blind from birth, in 1863 Fanny Crosby began to use her gift for writing poetry to compose hymns that have had a profound spiritual impact on countless people. She wrote so many—some eight thousand in all—that she had to use nearly a hundred pen names to get them all published; many are still sung today. And no name is more synonymous with turning small acts into big things for God than that of Mother Teresa, whose ministry to the poor of Calcutta is well known.

Many people could make a significant impact on the world, or the world around them, if they took small steps toward the work that God has given them to do. Harriet Beecher Stowe, Fanny Crosby, and Mother Teresa did not set out to change the world. But they also didn't give up because they considered their influence insignificant. They did what God wanted them to do, when he wanted them to do it. And he turned their seemingly small works into life-changing accomplishments—and

Eye has not seen, nor ear heard, nor have entered into the heart of man the things which God has prepared for those who love Him.

1 Corinthians 2:9 NKJV

he can do the same for you. Take those baby steps, and trust him with where they take you.

Follow God wherever he leads you, and leave the results of your work up to him. Your small acts of obedience may have a huge impact that you may never see.

what's essential

 When it comes to making a difference in the world, God is simply looking for people who will seek his guidance and follow his direction. All they need do is take the first steps, and he'll take it from there.

DO continue to dream of doing big things for God even as you are taking small steps of obedience.

DO ask "What can I do to help?" when you see a need that touches your heart.

DON'T let your feelings of insignificance prevent you from following God's leading.

DON'T focus on the potential impact of your work but rather on your immediate obedience to God.

Let His Love Overflow

God not only loves; he is love. But what does that mean? Scholars, theologians, and people like you have all sought to define "God is love." But it may be that the best definition is already found in a familiar Bible verse: "God so loved the world, that he gave his only Son" (John 3:16 ESV).

If you've ever felt at a loss for words—and who hasn't?—it may not be your fault at all. Your inability to express yourself adequately could result from the limitations of the English language. You need only look at the words "I love you" to recognize those limitations. That sentiment takes on a distinctly different meaning when it comes to the object of your affection. "I love you" hardly conveys the same meaning when you say it to your mother that it does when you say it to your husband or boyfriend. It doesn't even mean the same thing when you say it to your daughter or to a close friend. The English word *love* makes no distinction among the different kinds of affection you feel for the people in your life.

May the Lord make your love for each other and for everyone else grow by leaps and bounds. That's how our love for you has grown.

1 Thessalonians 3:12 CEV

Our hearts have been made to cry out for a love that can come only from our Creator. The cup of our soul will never be filled apart from the love of God.

Angela Thomas

Classic Greek does a much better job of linguistically separating diverse kinds of love. Four different words were used for *love;* the three most common referred to affection, friendship, and romance. The fourth word was seldom used until Jesus came to earth and became its living definition. That word is *agape* (pronounced uh-GAH-pay), and it has become so closely tied to Jesus that few people realize it is not a uniquely Christian word. Before Christ, it carried the connotation of having high regard, but once his followers started using *agape* to describe the love of God, the word took on a new meaning.

 We become what we love, and who we love shapes what we become . . . we are to become vessels of God's compassionate love for others.
—Saint Clare of Assisi

The apostle John intentionally used the word *agape* in John 3:16; no other Greek word came close to describing the profound love for humanity that compelled God to send his Son to the cross to suffer and die in one final, dramatic, sacrificial act to spare people from the consequences of their disobedience to God's laws. It's the same word John used in one of his letters, in which he wrote, "God is love" (1 John 4:8 NKJV).

But the most startling uses of the word *agape* occurred when Jesus and the New Testament writers told God's followers to love each other with this same *agape* love—the deep sacrificial love of God. "I am giving you a new commandment: Love each other,"

Jesus told his disciples during the last meal they would share together. "Just as I have loved you, you should love each other" (John 13:34 NLT). The love among his followers was to surpass the love shared among friends. In using the word *agape*, Jesus made it clear that they were to love God's family to the point of giving their lives for each other—whether they deserved that kind of sacrifice or not. "Just as I have loved you," Jesus said. Just as he sacrificed his life for you, whether you deserved it or not.

This is yet another reason God sent the Holy Spirit to earth—to so fill his people with his *agape* love that it would overflow from God's Spirit to others. He knows that this kind of love doesn't come naturally to people. Instead, he fills you to overflowing with his love. As *The Message* paraphrase expresses it, "We can't round up enough containers to hold everything God generously pours into our lives through the Holy Spirit!" (Romans 5:5). And that includes his love.

Be as generous with the love of God as he is. Let his love flow through you to the people in your life, even if you're not sure you think they deserve it. Allow his love to transform you and the world around you—your loved ones, your friends, your neighbors, your coworkers, and, yes, even your enemies. *Especially* your enemies. Just as Jesus' love did.

When you are filled with *agape,* loving even the unlovable people in your life becomes effortless. You begin to see them as God sees them—people who desperately need the love of God in their lives.

what's essential

 The love of God is a sacrificial love, as evidenced by Jesus' death on the cross. God wants you to have that same kind of love for everyone in his family. You can count on the Holy Spirit to give you more of God's love than you can possibly contain—more than enough to give away.

DO read passages from the Bible that talk about God's love, such as 1 Corinthians 13 and the first letter of John.

DO allow God's love to overflow from your life and into the lives of the people around you.

DON'T confuse God's profound *agape* love with affection, friendship, or romantic love.

DON'T make the mistake of thinking that you can't love the unlovable; with God's love, you can.

Faith

Because of his great love for us, God, who is rich in mercy, made us alive with Christ even when we were dead in transgressions—it is by grace you have been saved. And God raised us up with Christ and seated us with him in the heavenly realms in Christ Jesus, in order that in the coming ages he might show the incomparable riches of his grace, expressed in his kindness to us in Christ Jesus. For it is by grace you have been saved, through faith—and this not from yourselves, it is the gift of God—not by works, so that no one can boast.

Ephesians 2:4–9 NIV

You are a child of your heavenly Father. Your faith in his love and power can never be bold enough.

Basilea Schlink

Faith is the strength by which a shattered world shall emerge into the light.

Helen Keller

Express God's Joy

The joy we experience sometimes defies understanding. That's what's known as the joy of the Lord—what the apostle Peter described as "glorious, inexpressible joy" (1 Peter 1:8 NLT). It's the kind you can have under any circumstances, even when you must give up something you love with all your heart.

That's what Hannah, an Israelite woman who is mentioned in the Bible, had to do. She lived about a thousand years before the birth of Jesus, at a time when a woman's role and status in her culture depended on her ability to produce an heir for her husband. But Hannah was infertile, which allowed her husband, Elkanah, to take a second wife in the hopes that she would produce children.

Though he deeply loved Hannah, Elkanah married a woman named Peninnah, who bore him several children. Peninnah made life miserable for Hannah, taunting her about her infertility. Their story is told in the early chapters of the Bible book of 1 Samuel, which describes Hannah's anguish over her situation and her intense longing for a child of her own.

The young women will dance for joy, and the men—old and young—will join in the celebration. I will turn their mourning into joy. I will comfort them and exchange their sorrow for rejoicing.

Jeremiah 31:13 NLT

Joy seems to me a step beyond happiness—happiness is a sort of atmosphere you can live in sometimes when you're lucky. Joy is a light that fills you with hope and faith and love.

Adela Rogers St. Johns

One day her suffering nearly reached the breaking point. As she poured out her sorrow to God at the Shiloh temple north of Jerusalem, she made a vow to God that if he would give her a son, she would dedicate the child to serve in the tabernacle. That meant as soon as the child was no longer nursing, he would be taken to the temple to live so he could spend his life serving God and learning about him.

 People need joy as much as clothing. Some of them need it far more.
—Margaret Collier Graham

Eli, the priest at the temple, assured her that God would answer her prayer. And in due time, he did. Hannah gave birth to a son, whom she named Samuel, and as soon as he was weaned— in that culture, when he was two or three—she took him to Eli and reminded the priest of the vow she had made. Hannah and Elkanah left Samuel in the care of Eli.

Stop for a moment and think about how you might feel in a similar situation. You've experienced shame, humiliation, and ridicule. Finally—*finally*—you are blessed with that which will erase those negative emotions and experiences. And then you have to give up that blessing forever. You'd certainly be forgiven if joyfulness didn't describe your demeanor at the time. But it did for Hannah. Her immediate response upon leaving Samuel at the tabernacle was one of joyful praise to God. In her song of praise, found in 1 Samuel 2:1–10, Hannah expressed her joy at God's answer to her prayer.

The kind of joy Hannah experienced—the joy of the Lord— stemmed from her deep faith in God. The apostle Paul, who had just admitted that he wanted to die so he could be with Jesus, made the connection between joy and faith in Philippians 1:25: "I am convinced that I will remain alive so I can continue to help all of you grow and experience the joy of your faith" (NLT). Hannah's joy was also a result of her obedience; one of the psalmists made that connection clear: "Praise the LORD! How joyful are those who fear the LORD and delight in obeying his commands" (Psalm 112:1 NLT).

Ultimately, the joy of the Lord is a gift from God:

- You have filled my heart with greater joy than when their grain and new wine abound"(Psalm 4:7 NIV).

- "You have endowed him with eternal blessings and given him the joy of your presence" (Psalm 21:6 NLT).

- God gives wisdom, knowledge, and joy to those who please him" (Ecclesiastes 2:26 NLT).

- "I have given rest to the weary and joy to the sorrowing" (Jeremiah 31:25 NLT).

In the midst of sorrow, loss, disappointment, and a host of other difficult situations, you can experience God's gift of "glorious, inexpressible joy." The joy of the Lord is available to you today, as you exercise your faith and obedience—just as Hannah did.

interesting to note

The Bible records an incident in which the Jewish religious leaders, feeling threatened by the growth of the early church, rounded up the apostles and beat them. The result? The apostles "departed from the presence of the council, rejoicing that they were counted worthy to suffer shame for [Jesus'] name" (Acts 5:41 NKJV).

God had made the people very happy, and so on that day they celebrated and offered many sacrifices. The women and children joined in the festivities, and joyful shouts could be heard far from the city of Jerusalem.

Nehemiah 12:43 CEV

Praise is closely tied to joy. When you're in a difficult situation, begin to praise God in the middle of your pain, fear, sorrow, tears—whatever emotions you may be experiencing. Joy can break through every barrier, astonishing us with its presence when we least expect it.

what's essential

 Joy is a gift of God and a result of faith and obedience. It's not something you can manufacture. There's no need to pretend you're feeling joyful when you're not. God can and will provide the real thing, as you trust him, praise him, and rely on him to transform your sorrow into joy.

DO believe that no matter what your circumstances, you can experience the joy of the Lord.

DO begin to understand that authentic joy is ultimately a gift from God.

DON'T forget to praise God in the midst of every difficult situation in your life.

DON'T expect anything less than a pure, deep, abiding joy whenever you have to give up something you love for God.

Enjoy the Peace of God

Peace is a condition that can often seem to be in short supply, whether it's peace in the Middle East or peace in your own family. But there's one kind of peace that's available in an unlimited supply, and that's the peace that defies our under-standing—the peace of God.

O n the last night of his life on earth, Jesus spoke to his disciples about what would soon be happening to him. He would be departing from them, he said, but he would leave his disciples with the gift of peace, the kind of peace that only he could give. This peace was much more precious than mere freedom from conflict. This peace was an inner one that transcended every manner of conflict, turmoil, and difficulty.

The Bible describes this as a peace "that no one can completely understand" (Philippians 4:7 CEV). You've likely seen examples of it and maybe even experienced it yourself. An inexplicable calm as-sures you everything will be all right even when all around you there's nothing but evidence to the contrary. Your car needs a new transmission and

I am leaving you with a gift—peace of mind and heart. And the peace I give is a gift the world cannot give. So don't be troubled or afraid.

John 14:27 NLT

When you at last give your life—bringing into alignment your beliefs and the way you live—then, and only then, can you begin to find inner peace.

Peace Pilgrim

you can't get to work, but if you don't go to work you won't be able to get the transmission fixed. Sometimes in situations like that, a peace that defies logic may overtake you despite your best efforts to worry. That's the peace of God at work in your life. Jesus left this gift behind when he gave up his life on earth. Best of all, you can have this gift all the time, not just "sometimes."

 Peace reigns where our Lord reigns.
—Julian of Norwich

That may seem like a stretch, but it isn't. The Bible offers assurance that God will give you what the book of Isaiah calls "perfect" peace: "You will keep in perfect peace all who trust in you, all whose thoughts are fixed on you!" (26:3 NLT). But what does Isaiah mean by "perfect" peace? The most obvious answer is that because God is perfect, his peace is perfect. There's more, though. His peace is perfect because it can overcome every single thing that threatens to create havoc or tension in your life. The peace of God is greater than any problem, difficulty, or even tragedy. His peace won't change the situation itself, but it will change *you* in the midst of the situation.

His peace is also perfect because of its unlimited supply. Because God is eternal and infinite, so is his peace. You can never use up your allotment of God's peace, because there is no allotment. Think about that—God's peace will be available to you every day, in every circumstance, in an unlimited supply, for the rest of your life! That's worth getting excited about!

Before you get too excited, though, look at Isaiah 26:3 again; you do bear some responsibility in accessing God's peace. You have to trust God and keep your mind on him all the time. That first condition makes sense; the peace of God would seem to be a natural consequence of trusting him. But keeping your thoughts "fixed" on him? How can you possibly fulfill that condition? How can you think about God all the time?

Rest assured, not even Isaiah thought only about God. What Isaiah is saying is that God will extend his peace to any person whose mind is so dedicated to God that her thoughts immediately turn to him in every circumstance. You hear rumors of layoffs where you work; your thoughts turn to God. Your friend is diagnosed with breast cancer; your thoughts turn to God. Your neighbor's daughter runs away yet again; your thoughts turn to God.

Your God-centered thoughts reflect an orientation of your mind, just as your trust in God reflects an orientation of your heart. Keep your mind and your heart oriented toward God, and his perfect peace, the peace that no one completely understands, will control the way you think and feel.

In the midst of difficult situations, fear can rob you of your peace. When you feel that start to

interesting to note

The peace of God once had a secondary meaning. In medieval times, the term referred to a cultural understanding that in time of war, church buildings, the clergy, women, pilgrims, and the poor were never to be attacked. Violators would be excommunicated, or banned, from the church.

I pray that God will be kind to you and will let you live in perfect peace! May you keep learning more and more about God and our Lord Jesus.

2 Peter 1:2 CEV

happen, turn to God immediately and ask him to replace your fear with his perfect peace. Keep your thoughts on him, trusting him to fill your life with the peace that only he can give.

what's essential

 Placing your trust in God and keeping your thoughts turned in his direction are essential conditions for the peace of God to reign over your life. As you orient your life toward God, his perfect peace will permeate every aspect of your life.

DO trust God to give you his perfect peace by keeping your heart and mind oriented toward him.

DO understand that God's peace can overcome every circumstance in your life.

DON'T think that if you ask for God's peace too often, you'll use up your quota; his peace is in endless supply.

DON'T allow fear to rob you of your peace; ask God to replace your fear with his perfect peace.

Seek the Strength to Endure

Patience. Perseverance. Endurance. Not exactly words you tend to associate with living the abundant life Jesus promised, a life filled with joy and peace and every other wonderful gift from God. But the strength to withstand difficulties is as wonderful a gift as any other that God has given you.

You need to persevere so that when you have done the will of God, you will receive what he has promised.

Hebrews 10:36 NIV

I t's a rare woman who hasn't felt overwhelmed by the circumstances of her life. You've probably felt that way at different times, times when you wondered if you had the emotional strength to survive another day. It doesn't help that instant gratification has nearly become the norm in much of the world. Whether it's movies on demand, lightning-fast Internet connections, equally fast computer processors, or faster-than-ever fast food, people want what they want *now*. That demand for speed sometimes carries over to your personal life; having to wait for all to be right in the world isn't on the agenda.

But major difficulties rarely get resolved overnight, and persevering through them strengthens

Strength is born in the deep silence of long-suffering hearts.

Felicia Hemans

your character and your faith in God. Trusting God over the long haul elevates your steely determination—often evidenced by your clenched jaw—to the level of hope-filled expectation. That expectation may be accompanied by many tears, but the hope is there nonetheless.

The Bible even says you should consider seemingly endless difficulties to be a blessing. The apostle James wrote this: "Consider it a sheer gift, friends, when tests and challenges come at you from all sides. You know that under pressure, your faith-life is forced into the open and shows its true colors. So don't try to get out of anything prematurely. Let it do its work so you become mature and well-developed, not deficient in any way" (James 1:2–4 MSG). That may not be the advice you want to hear, but it is sound advice if you want to experience all that God has for you.

Nothing great was ever done without much enduring.
—Saint Catherine of Siena

One biblical woman in particular epitomizes the value of persevering. Sarah lived in present-day Iraq in Ur, a city of great wealth and culture. But she and her husband, Abraham, followed God's direction and left Ur for parts unknown, to fulfill God's promise that Abraham would become the "father of many nations." Abraham was seventy-five, Sarah sixty-six. They had no children; Sarah's barrenness had been a source of shame for her for at least five decades.

Scholars say that at the time, women experienced menopause at a much later age than women today. Sarah likely reached menopause when she was about seventy-five. She realized she could not help Abraham fulfill God's promise, so she urged him to have children by her servant, Hagar. Not the best move, to be sure, but those who criticize Sarah for intervening need to realize that she persevered from the time she married Abraham—perhaps as early as age twelve—until the onset of menopause. That's sixty-three years of waiting, first to simply conceive a child and later to see God's promise fulfilled through conceiving many children.

Sarah learned a hard lesson about interfering with God's plans, but she eventually gave birth to a son, Isaac, when she was ninety years old— long past menopause. The book of Hebrews credits her with trusting God to the end: "Even when Sarah was too old to have children, she had faith that God would do what he had promised, and she had a son. Her husband Abraham was almost dead, but he became the ancestor of many people. In fact, there are as many of them as there are stars in the sky or grains of sand along the beach" (Hebrews 11:11–12 CEV).

Perseverance isn't easy, nor is it fun. It's probably not something you anticipated when you signed on to this new way of living. But the rewards of patiently enduring the difficult situations in your life, trusting God through all the setbacks and frustrations and pain, can't be overstated. God's blessings make it all worthwhile.

Just as you can build up your physical endurance, you can build up your emotional stamina. Practicing patience and perseverance in the minor irritations in life—trusting in God even in those situations—helps you learn to endure greater difficulties.

what's essential

 Endurance strengthens both your character and your trust in God. As you persevere through hardship, your faith gets a workout, building up your ability to withstand whatever challenges life throws at you.

DO recognize your ability to endure hardship for the gift that it is.

DO allow God to transform your steely determination into hope-filled expectation.

DON'T expect major difficulties to be resolved quickly.

DON'T give up prematurely; the rewards God has for you may be closer than you think.

Wear Kindness and Compassion

What woman doesn't love to be well-dressed? A perfectly tailored outfit in just the right style and color can make you feel wonderful. Your mood changes, your spirits are lifted, and your whole demeanor brightens. Well, good news! God has created a wardrobe for you that does all that and more.

See if this sounds familiar. You're in a fine-dining restaurant for a special occasion, and as you look around the room, your eyes are drawn to one woman in particular. She looks exactly the way you wish you looked—impeccably decked out in a beautiful dress in a style that flatters her enviable figure and a color that perfectly complements her sapphire-blue eyes. You sigh, wishing for all the world that you could look that good just once in your life.

And then, she opens her mouth to speak. She berates her date for failing to get a reservation at the restaurant she wanted to go to. Nothing on the menu meets with her approval, and she lets everyone within earshot know it. She nitpicks over everything—the garlic butter with the escargot, the

> Chosen by God for this new life of love, dress in the wardrobe God picked out for you: compassion, kindness, humility, quiet strength, discipline . . . And regardless of what else you put on, wear love. It's your basic, all-purpose garment. Never be without it.
>
> **Colossians 3:12, 14**
> MSG

> A single act of kindness throws out roots in all directions, and the roots spring up and make new trees. The greatest work that kindness does to others is that it makes them kind themselves.
>
> **Amelia Earhart**

temperature of the lobster bisque, the doneness of the steak au poivre—as her date squirms in embarrassment. By the time dessert arrives, she's no longer that flawless woman you envied an hour before. Her attitude has revealed her inner nature, and it's anything but beautiful. Her appearance is no longer attractive.

God is the ultimate Designer, and the wardrobe God has selected for you ensures that you will always be among the best-dressed women in any crowd. That's because the wardrobe he created for you is the kind that clothes you with inner beauty. It will always be in style, fit your budget, and complement your personality.

 Love and kindness are never wasted. They always make a difference. They bless the one who receives them, and they bless you, the giver. —Barbara De Angelis

Take a look at the various pieces that God has included in a versatile ensemble that works for everyday use, special events, and any other occasion you can think of:

Compassion. When you clothe yourself with godly compassion, you feel the misery and despair of others as if you were experiencing it yourself. Your tenderhearted concern for another person's condition runs so deep that you share in her suffering.

Kindness. Here's what distinguishes God's brand of kindness from every other type. He wants you to treat your enemies with the same measure of kindness that you extend to the people you love the most. And you're to be just as kind in private as you are in public, just as kind in your private thoughts as you are in your public words and actions.

Humility. In a sense, humility is the foundation for kindness and compassion. Humility exhibits no trace of arrogance or pretension; it's a quality that says "You first" in every interaction with other people. When you wear a garment of genuine humility, you shine the spotlight on others—never on yourself.

Quiet strength. Think of a woman you know who has poise and confidence. She's an example of quiet strength—a composed, tranquil nature. Clothe all that in God's strength, and you have a woman whose serenity has a calming effect on everyone around her.

Discipline. This element in your wardrobe shows that you have self-control. In relation to humility, kindness, and compassion, your disciplined nature restrains you from acting in a way that is contrary to those three qualities.

Love. Yes, this truly is your "all-purpose garment." When you wear love, you wear the masterpiece of God's design. Love is the piece of your ensemble that makes a statement like no other. This garment says to the rest of the world, "You are far more important than I am. How can I serve you today?"

Do you want to always be the best-dressed woman in the room? Clothe yourself in a way that

interesting to note

God has also created a special-purpose wardrobe for you. The Bible calls it the full armor of God, and it includes such components as truth, justice, peace, faith, and salvation—everything you need for protection from anything that tries to get between you and God. You can read about it in Ephesians 6:10–18

Be kind and compassionate to one another, forgiving each other, just as in Christ God forgave you.

Ephesians 4:32 NIV

represents your new life—with compassion, kindness, humility, quiet strength, discipline, and love.

As you check your appearance in the mirror each time you leave the house, check your attitude as well. Are you clothed in the outfit God has created for you? If so, good for you! You're about to make your world a better place, in your own small but significant way.

what's essential

 Kindness and compassion—along with humility, quiet strength, discipline, and love—provide the foundation for the best makeover you'll ever have. Clothing yourself in those qualities automatically and immediately improves your appearance—and your life.

DO consider the elements of a wardrobe designed by God to be much more important than an outfit from any other designer.

DO make sure that your personality and actions are a positive reflection of your new life with God.

DON'T ruin your appearance by exhibiting behavior that is contrary to that which pleases God.

DON'T keep your inner beauty from shining through by blocking it with a negative attitude.

Grow in Your Faith

At some point in your relationship with God, you will likely hear someone ask if you are growing in your faith—and you may wonder what they're talking about. How do you grow in your faith? How can you tell if you're growing in your faith? How do you know when your faith is all grown up?

Think about some of the things that help you grow in a healthy way—good nutrition, exercise, fresh air, positive relationships, meaningful work, and so forth. Those elements, along with many others, contribute to your emotional, intellectual, and physical growth. Spiritual growth also requires certain elements to help you grow strong in your faith in God. Without them, your faith would stagnate, and you would spend your life at square one, never moving forward.

So how do you grow in your faith? Making the following practices a regular part of your life will help you grow toward maturity in your faith:

Prayer. The importance of regular prayer is vital to a healthy life of faith. Prayer exercises your

> Let the wonderful kindness and the understanding that come from our Lord and Savior Jesus Christ help you to keep on growing. Praise Jesus now and forever! Amen.
>
> **2 Peter 3:18** CEV

> Some tension is necessary for the soul to grow, and we can put that tension to good use. We can look for every opportunity to give and receive love, to appreciate nature, to heal our wounds and the wounds of others, to forgive, and to serve.
>
> **Joan Borysenko**

faith muscles by increasing your faith when God answers your prayers. And it keeps you connected with God through daily conversations and a mind and a heart that are oriented toward him throughout the day.

Bible reading. Reading the Bible not only teaches you about God and his purposes for humanity but it also offers comfort, assurance, encouragement, hope, peace, and so much more. Read the Bible to learn, but also read it to grow.

In this word, things that are naturally to endure for a long time are the slowest in reaching maturity.
—Saint Vincent de Paul

Fellowship. Many followers of Jesus use that word when they talk about getting together with other people of like mind and faith. In one way, fellowship is similar to gravitating toward other knitters if you're a knitter yourself. But in another way, it's very different. Other knitters may teach you a new stitch or two, but other followers of God will walk alongside you as you navigate your way through life, in all its complexity and mystery, sharing in your sorrows, joys, pleasures, confusion, and, well, everything else.

Journaling. Women are especially drawn to journaling, and it's likely that you already do some form of journaling. Use this special time to pour out your heart to God, and expect him to speak to you as you do. Weeks, months, even years later, when you go back and read what you've written, you may be astonished to discover the depth of wisdom you acquire through what seems to be a simple practice.

Serving others. You may be amazed at how dramatically your life can change for the better when you get out and start serving other people. You may also be amazed at the many ways you can be of service. Churches would not exist without the help of volunteers, but you can also grow in your faith by volunteering in your community. Hospice, search-and-rescue organizations, homeless shelters, soup kitchens, thrift stores run by nonprofits—these areas and many more rely on people who have a heart for serving others.

Reading books. There's no lack of books on the market that can help you grow in your faith. Many books dedicated specifically to spiritual living and growth are available in Christian and secular bookstores. In addition, religious fiction can be a powerful element in helping you grow in your faith. Ask friends whose spiritual maturity you respect to recommend some specific titles.

So, how can you tell if you're growing in your faith? If you follow practices such as the ones just listed, you are. You don't need to worry about where you are on some arbitrary spiritual-growth scale; God will nudge you along if you start to stagnate.

And how do you know when your faith is all grown up? Your faith won't be all grown up until

interesting to note

Many people have grown in their faith by going on a pilgrimage. You don't have to visit Jerusalem to experience pilgrimage; you can start by visiting cathedrals or other worship centers near where you live— not as a sightseer, but as a follower of God who wants to experience him in a new and unfamiliar environment.

Like newborn babies, crave pure spiritual milk, so that by it you may grow up in your salvation, now that you have tasted that the Lord is good.
1 Peter 2:2–3 NIV

you are in the presence of God in eternity. That's when you reach full spiritual maturity. In the meantime, keep growing in your faith in this life.

Be sure to put into practice the activities that will lead to spiritual growth, but remember to relax and enjoy the process. Spiritual maturity takes time. Become immersed in the things that will bring you closer to God, fully appreciating them rather than trying to gauge your growth.

what's essential

 Any practice that helps you grow in your faith is worth devoting time to. That may mean replacing activities that were once important to you with things like reading your Bible more often. In time, you'll see that the benefits far outweigh the adjustments you may need to make in the way you spend your time.

DO explore the various practices you can incorporate into your daily life in order to grow in your faith.

DO enlist the help of others who follow God to help you become more mature spiritually.

DON'T get hung up on wondering whether you are growing or growing fast enough.

DON'T expect to reach a point in your faith where you no longer feel the need to continue growing.

Church

He [Christ] is far above any ruler or authority or power or leader or anything else—not only in this world but also in the world to come. God has put all things under the authority of Christ and has made him head over all things for the benefit of the church. And the church is his body; it is made full and complete by Christ, who fills all things everywhere with himself.

Ephesians 1:21–23 NLT

The church is the great lost and found department.

Robert Short

When we worship together as a community of living Christians, we do not worship alone, we worship "with all the company of heaven."

Marianne H. Micks

Be Trustworthy

What kind of person do you think of when you hear the word trustworthy? Perhaps you think of a good friend, a member of the clergy, or a leader in your community. How about a prostitute? Not a lot of people would apply that description to such a woman, but the Bible does.

[Paul wrote:] You have heard me teach things that have been confirmed by many reliable witnesses. Now teach these truths to other trustworthy people who will be able to pass them on to others.

2 Timothy 2:2 NLT

That woman was named Rahab, and her story is found in Joshua 2. Under the leadership of Joshua, the Israelites were poised to enter the promised land—the land that God had told them they could possess. Joshua sent out spies to determine what kind of challenges the Israelites would face in attempting to conquer the area. Two of the spies had taken refuge in Rahab's home in Jericho in enemy territory.

Word got out that the spies were there, and the king demanded that Rahab deliver them to him. She denied knowing where they were, even though they were hiding out on her roof. Why would she do that? Had the spies been found in her home, Rahab could have been put to death. But Rahab considered something else to be of greater

When there is strong trust, a person tends to be more open and less defensive. He doesn't have to spend time proving something. Facades can drop and be replaced with directness and honesty.

Ted W. Engstrom

importance: the truth of God. Rahab believed that the Israelites' God was the one true God. She told the spies, "The LORD your God is the supreme God of the heavens above and the earth below" (Joshua 2:11 NLT).

By that point, Rahab had proven herself to be trustworthy. So when she told the spies how they could escape, they didn't hesitate. They knew they could trust her instructions.

Your faithfulness makes you trustworthy to God.
—Edwin Louis Cole

Being a trustworthy person has nothing to do with the job you hold, your standing in the community, or the church you attend—if you even attend church at all. But it has everything to do with your proven character. You earn the right and privilege of being considered trustworthy by proving over and over again that you are a person of integrity who can be counted on to do the right thing. That includes doing what you say you'll do, keeping your commitments, following God faithfully, and remaining loyal to your friends and family.

It also includes keeping a confidence, something the Bible singles out as an example of trustworthiness: "A gossip goes around telling secrets, but those who are trustworthy can keep a confidence" (Proverbs 11:13 NLT). Few women think of themselves as gossips; gossiping is something other women do, not themselves. After all, it's not as if they rush to the phone to spread the news about a brewing scandal. They'd never do that, so how could they be considered gossips? Easily. Any woman who

The trustworthy person will get a rich reward, but a person who wants quick riches will get into trouble.

Proverbs 28:20 NLT

shares her concerns about a problem in a neighbor's family is a gossip. So is anyone who betrays a confidence by soliciting help in determining how to pray for the person who confided in her. What about someone who didn't know she wasn't supposed to repeat something a friend told her? The reality is that most of the time, people know better than to repeat a story; using the "no one told me not to" defense is a flimsy excuse at best.

Trustworthy people don't skate right up to the line between right and wrong. They keep their distance on the side of right, never wondering how far they can go before crossing over into wrong territory. Someone shares a confidence with them, and that's the end of it; they repeat it to no one except to God in private prayer. Trustworthy people don't make a commitment and then try to figure out how to get out of it; they follow through with the commitment no matter how inconvenient it turns out to be for them.

To God, trustworthy people are those he knows he can count on to follow through with the responsibilities he has given them. They've proven themselves by following him faithfully. They're people like Rahab, who proved herself so trustworthy that God bestowed on her an exceptional honor: a place in the lineage of Jesus, according to Matthew 1:5.

You can start to become more trustworthy by tackling one area of your life at a time. If you're habitually late, for instance, practice being on time until it becomes second nature to you. Apply this same procedure to other areas where you feel you may fall short with regard to your complete trustworthiness.

what's essential

 A trustworthy person is one whom God and other people can trust to do the right thing in every situation. She's a person who can be given increasing responsibility, confided in with confidence, and counted on to follow through with the commitments she has made.

DO consider trustworthiness a trait to be cultivated in your life.

DO act on the side of caution when it comes to repeating information that could be considered confidential.

DON'T use the wrong criteria, such as a person's standing in the community, to determine whether he or she can be trusted.

DON'T fail to follow through on your commitments, no matter how inconvenient it may be for you.

Forgive Others

For all of humanity's attempts to reduce God to an indulgent grandfather, a generous Santa Claus, or a ruthless judge in the sky, God has always been and will always be beyond human comprehension. And when it comes to his radical forgiveness, he proves just how far outside the scope of human understanding he exists.

When you have a serious grievance against someone, the last thing you probably want to hear is that you need to forgive him. Everything in you may rebel against that notion: *Why should I forgive him? He should apologize to me!* And maybe he should. But your responsibility is to forgive. Why? Because that's what God wants you to do. Because it frees you from the burden of carting around all that unforgiveness. Because it changes you on the inside, and that in turn changes the way you live your life on the outside.

Once you're convinced that you *should* forgive, though, a second set of questions emerges: *How on earth can I ever forgive him? I don't have it in me to do that! His betrayal was too painful!* Well, God also has the answer to those questions, and he provided them in one of the most bewildering books in the entire Bible, the book of the prophet Hosea.

If you've ever read Hosea, you may have found yourself reading certain sections over again, because you couldn't believe you read it right the first time through. And then you discover that yes, God really did command Hosea to find a prostitute, marry her, have children with her, and continue to take her back no matter how often she returned to her questionable profession: "Start all over: Love your wife again, your wife who's in bed with her latest boyfriend, your cheating wife" (3:1 MSG).

 Forgiveness is almost a selfish act because of its immense benefits to the one who forgives.
—Lawana Blackwell

Mind you, God wasn't punishing Hosea for some egregious indiscretion on his part. No, Hosea was a prophet in good standing with God. That fact was that Hosea himself was practically irrelevant in this drama that God was directing. Hosea's role was symbolic; he was standing in for God, while his wife, Gomer, represented Israel. Israel had turned from God and cheated on him by pursuing other gods—the false gods of the surrounding nations.

Through Hosea's relentless forgiveness of his cheating wife, God was showing the unfaithful nation of Israel his own divine,

Correct any followers of mine who sin, and forgive the ones who say they are sorry. Even if one of them mistreats you seven times in one day and says, "I am sorry," you should still forgive that person.

Luke 17:3–4 CEV

supernatural love and forgiveness. Toward the end of this drama, God made this promise: "I will love them lavishly. My anger is played out. I will make a fresh start with Israel" (14:4–5 MSG).

So here's how you can forgive someone who has hurt you deeply: you follow the principle of forgiveness exemplified by Hosea's example. Does that mean you have to allow a betrayer back into your life? Only if God tells you to, as he did with Hosea. Your responsibility is to follow the principle of loving and forgiving the person with God's supernatural power.

You say you still don't have it in you to do that? Actually, you do, if you have the Holy Spirit in your life. He provides all the power you need to truly forgive another person. And it's clear from the teachings of Jesus that God expects you to forgive as he forgave. Forgive other people over and over again, Jesus said, and don't even approach God in worship until you have done so. Jesus never gave people an easy out when it came to forgiveness.

God modeled forgiveness through the story of Hosea. Jesus modeled forgiveness when he cried out on the cross, "Father, forgive them, for they do not know what they are doing" (Luke 23:34 NIV). But ordinary people also model forgiveness, from the survivors of the 2007 massacre at

Virginia Tech to many who have lost loved ones in Iraq and Afghanistan. It may be beyond the scope of our understanding, but radical forgiveness is possible—even for humans.

As God reminds you of people you need to forgive, meditate on God's forgiveness of you. Recalling and appreciating his gracious forgiveness can go a long way toward transforming your attitude toward someone who has hurt you.

what's essential

 Forgiveness can be a difficult process, but it's an essential one. God expects his people to be a forgiving people, drawing on Jesus' teachings on forgiveness, his own modeling of forgiveness, and the Holy Spirit's power.

DO follow God's example of forgiveness, and be a model of forgiveness for others to follow.

DO rely on the power of the Holy Spirit working in your life to enable you to forgive someone who has betrayed you.

DON'T ignore Jesus' relentless teachings on the way God expects his people to forgive others.

DON'T forget that harboring an attitude of unforgiveness is harmful to both your spiritual life and your health.

Cultivate Humility

When it comes to women who are models of humility, you'd be hard-pressed to come up with a rival for Mary, the mother of Jesus. In fact, based on the Bible record of her life, Mary probably could not have imagined the adulation she would receive over the next two millennia.

Mary of Nazareth, a young girl of humble origins, was astonished when the angel of God greeted her as the "highly favored" one (Luke 1:28 NIV). It's likely that she never thought of herself as anyone special and could not fathom what she had done to warrant this special visitation.

Then the angel announced that she would give birth to the long-awaited Messiah. Mary accepted the news with remarkable grace and simple faith, two components of humility. Her response is so subdued that you can almost see her bowing as she responds: "I am the Lord's servant. May it be to me as you have said" (Luke 1:38 NIV). And then, just as you'd expect of a girl of about thirteen years of age, Mary ran to share the news with an older cousin, Elizabeth, who was pregnant with John—the one who would come to be known as John the Baptist.

One thing that's striking so far in this story is that there's no indication that Mary shared the news with anyone else. Imagine receiving that kind of news and keeping it private; if that happened to a woman today, you'd expect her announcement to be the next big viral video on YouTube and her tweets to offer up-to-the-minute pregnancy news on Twitter. But even after the angels announced the birth of Jesus and the shepherds came running to worship him, Mary remained quiet and restrained: "Mary kept all these things to herself, holding them dear, deep within herself," according to Luke 2:19 (MSG).

 It is no great thing to be humble when you are brought low; but to be humble when you are praised is a great and rare attainment. —Saint Bernard of Clairvaux

Years later when a very young Jesus amazed the temple scholars with his scriptural wisdom, Mary once again "held these things dearly, deep within herself" (Luke 2:51 MSG). The Bible, which hardly avoids pointing out human flaws, never shows Mary trying to one-up the other mothers, bragging about her son the biblical scholar—or her son the Messiah. Even when Jesus began his public ministry, Mary simply blended in with the other female disciples.

Mary was given the greatest privilege ever bestowed on a human being but was content to live in her son's shadow. From what

interesting to note

Humility is considered by many biblical scholars to be the foundation for all other positive attributes, arguing that such qualities as love, faith, compassion, peace, and even joy are impossible to attain outside the framework of humility.

we know of her, she never drew attention to herself, never boasted about the favor God showed her, never expected special treatment, and never asserted any special authority as the mother of the Messiah. She was a model of humility who never exhibited any pride in what others surely recognized as her special status.

You don't have to be the mother of the Messiah to be a model of humility. Women who demonstrate humility are those who have found their identities in God and thus a contentment in the people God made them to be. They've humbled themselves before God, recognized his authority in their lives, and yielded their lives to him. Whatever he wants is fine with them. They'll work behind the scenes, play a supporting role, or step into the spotlight if that's what God requires of them. It doesn't matter, because all the praise goes to God anyway.

Humility's counterpart, pride, is among the most insidious character flaws because it can blind us to its very existence. It's difficult to root out because it runs so deep; we can see our dishonesty, for example, much more clearly than our pride, which is the cause of many of our other defects. We need to humble ourselves before God, ask the Holy Spirit to illuminate the dark corners of our nature where we've allowed pride to lurk, and then ask the Spirit to teach us to walk in humility as Mary did.

Whoever exalts himself will be humbled, and whoever humbles himself will be exalted.

Matthew 23:12 NIV

When you begin to focus on the quality of humility, you'll suddenly begin to recognize all those ugly, prideful thoughts and attitudes that you've been harboring. Don't be discouraged; that's a sign that the Holy Spirit truly is shining light on your pride so it can be transformed into humility.

what's essential

 People who are truly humble never think of themselves that way; they're too humble to acknowledge such a positive trait in themselves. Humility is such an integral part of their nature that they're unaware of it. It's just a part of who they are.

DO emulate the humble way Mary carried herself throughout her extraordinary life.

DO humble yourself before God and ask him to help you root out any pride in your character.

DON'T resist becoming the person God wants you to be by asserting yourself in inappropriate, prideful ways.

DON'T draw attention to yourself or your accomplishments; let God shine the light on you— if he so chooses.

Live on Purpose

As a woman, you know what it's like to go through the day on autopilot. It may not happen all the time, but when it does, you crawl into bed at night and wonder, Is this really living? You know the answer—no, it isn't—but you don't know what to do about it. As always, God is there to help you out.

What you need to do is permanently shut off the autopilot control and put yourself back in control of your life. As a follower of God, you realize that God is ultimately in control, but you still have a lot of navigating to do—and that means you have to pay closer attention than you did when autopilot was engaged.

Paying closer attention is a critical aspect of what has come to be called "living on purpose" or "living intentionally." When you begin to live intentionally, your actions take on greater significance, because you've made a conscious decision to take those actions. You're no longer carried along by circumstances or situations that are beyond your control.

One example is your schedule. It's not uncommon for women to be involved in myriad activities that once seemed like a good idea. But too often, even when those activities no longer serve a valid purpose, many women continue participating. Because they're operating on autopilot, their lives have become cluttered with meaningless time wasters. And they wonder why their very full lives seem so very empty.

 Lean forward into your life. Begin each day as if it were on purpose. —Mary Anne Radmacher

So how do you start living on purpose? Not surprisingly, the first step is to simply start paying attention to everything—your actions, your thoughts, and your emotions, of course, but also everything that's going on around you. This involves a significant shift in your way of thinking and living, because it requires you to live in the present moment. You may think you're already living in the present—where else *could* you live?—but once you begin to bring the present moment into sharp focus, you become acutely aware of how often your thoughts are consumed by the past and the future.

When you intentionally live in the present moment, you're finally free to focus on other people. You're no longer distracted by thoughts about what you have to do next, or tomorrow, or next week. Your complete focus is on what's happening *right now*—and if *right now* you're in the presence of other people, those people will feel as if they're important to you, maybe even special.

Look at the way Jesus lived. He lived his entire life intentionally. He knew his purpose and lived every moment in accordance with that purpose. And he encouraged others to do the same. One of the best-known passages in the New Testament—Matthew 6:24–34—records what he said about focused living. "No one can serve two masters, for either he will hate the one and love the other, or he will be devoted to the one and despise the other," he said (v. 24 ESV). In context, Jesus was talking about trying to serve God while trying to serve money, but the principle carries over to every area of life.

Jesus then described the things people waste their time worrying about—what they will eat or drink or wear—and how God will provide those things for people whose lives are focused on him. Look at what he said next: "Steep your life in God-reality, God-initiative, God-provisions. Don't worry about missing out. You'll find all your everyday human concerns will be met. Give your entire attention to what God is doing right now, and don't get worked up about what may or may not happen tomorrow. God will help you deal with whatever hard things come up when the time comes" (vv. 33–34 MSG).

That's living in the moment, living on purpose, and living intentionally, all wrapped up in two short verses of the Bible. And Jesus said you can do it. Disengage autopilot, start paying attention—and begin to truly live.

In Matthew 6:34 Jesus told his followers to focus on what God is doing at any given moment. You can train yourself to think that way by maintaining a close connection with God throughout the day. Stay focused on him, and he will let you know how he is working in your life at that time.

what's essential

 It's essential to understand that living intentionally simplifies your life rather than complicating it. It may seem difficult at first to train yourself to live in the moment, but once it becomes second nature to you, your life will take on a much more natural rhythm.

DO train your mind to focus on the present moment and what God is doing in that moment.

DO pay close attention to your actions, thoughts, and emotions and how they affect the way you spend your time.

DON'T give in to the temptation to go through your life on autopilot once you've turned the autopilot control off.

DON'T worry about tomorrow; God will take care of you no matter what comes your way.

Change Your Attitude

One day you go shopping for a suit you need for a conference you've been dreading; you have an utterly miserable time at the mall. A week later, you're back at the mall in search of an outfit for a friend's dinner party, and you have a wonderful time shopping. What changed? Mostly, your attitude.

Your attitude makes a huge difference in the way you approach the events in your life and in the way you interact with the people in your life. A negative attitude can make a promising day turn abysmal, while a positive attitude can turn a terrible day into a decent one. It all depends on your perspective—and the condition of your heart.

Your heart is where your attitudes take root and start to grow. You can try to cultivate a positive attitude on the outside, but if your inner attitude—your heart attitude—remains negative, you'll experience a constant tension between what's really on the inside and what you're trying to project on the outside. God, of course, can see right through you, and a surprising number of people can do the same.

A positive attitude is much more than a superficial smile on your face. A genuine positive attitude reflects what's deep inside you. And if your life is committed to God, then what's inside you are those positive attitudes that reflect his nature. What are those attributes? Some of them are what's known as the "fruit of the Spirit": love, joy, peace, patience, kindness, goodness, faithfulness, gentleness, and self-control. Here's how one Bible version describes those attributes: "What happens when we live God's way? He brings gifts into our lives, much the same way that fruit appears in an orchard—things like affection for others, exuberance about life, serenity. We develop a willingness to stick with things, a sense of compassion in the heart, and a conviction that a basic holiness permeates things and people. We find ourselves involved in loyal commitments, not needing to force our way in life, able to marshal and direct our energies wisely" (Galatians 5:22–23 MSG).

 God often comforts us, not by changing the circumstances of our lives, but by changing our attitude toward them.
—S. H. B. Masterman

Can you see how those qualities contribute to a positive attitude toward life? Here are some other godly attributes that create positive attitudes: humility, compassion, selflessness, loyalty, caring, encouragement, respect, impartiality, helpfulness, forgiveness—and many others. Identifying those attributes, however, is one thing; making them your own is quite another.

Have this mind among yourselves, which is yours in Christ Jesus, who, though he was in the form of God, did not count equality with God a thing to be grasped.

Philippians 2:5–6 ESV

How can you develop these qualities in order to cultivate a positive attitude? By now you know that every positive change in your life begins with God. Here's a verse that will help you rein in those thoughts that lead to a negative attitude: "We destroy arguments and every lofty opinion raised against the knowledge of God, and take every thought captive to obey Christ" (2 Corinthians 10:5 ESV). When you bring "every thought captive," you filter each thought through your understanding of God. A seemingly innocuous thought can prove to be a selfish one when filtered through your knowledge of God. Then it can be transformed into a godly, selfless attitude.

Meditating on Scripture and memorizing Bible verses are two great ways to cultivate a positive attitude. The Bible offers a specific way of doing this: "Summing it all up, friends, I'd say you'll do best by filling your minds and meditating on things true, noble, reputable, authentic, compelling, gracious—the best, not the worst; the beautiful, not the ugly; things to praise, not things to curse. Put into practice what you learned from me, what you heard and saw and realized. Do that, and God, who makes everything work together, will work you into his most excellent harmonies" (Philippians 4:8–9 MSG).

Finally—and this may be your biggest challenge—resist the efforts of other people to bring you down. Maintain your positive outlook, and trust God to let your demeanor point those other people to the source of your positive attitudes, God himself.

Catch yourself every time you allow a negative thought to affect your actions. The more you do this, the more you realize how much you need to adopt God's attributes in your life. Meditate on those attributes, and make them your own.

what's essential

 Your attitude can make all the difference in your day. Commit each day to God and ask him to keep your attitude in line with his.

DO give your negative thoughts over to God and allow him to transform them into their godly counterparts.

DO meditate on Scripture in order to keep your mind focused on those things that are pleasing to God.

DON'T let negative attitudes take root in your heart.

DON'T let other people rob you of the positive attitude you have toward life.

Prayer

When you pray, don't be like those show-offs who love to stand up and pray in the meeting places and on the street corners. They do this just to look good. I can assure you that they already have their reward. When you pray, go into a room alone and close the door. Pray to your Father in private. He knows what is done in private, and he will reward you. When you pray, don't talk on and on as people do who don't know God. They think God likes to hear long prayers. Don't be like them. Your Father knows what you need before you ask.

Matthew 6:5–8 CEV

The purpose of all prayer is to find God's will and to make that will our prayer.

Catherine Marshall

We must pray literally without ceasing—without ceasing; in every occurrence and employment of our lives. I mean that prayer of the heart which is independent of place or situation, or which is, rather, a habit of lifting up the heart to God, as in a constant communication with Him.

Saint Elizabeth Ann Seton

Watch What You Say

Look back over the course of your life. What has caused you more trouble more often—what you've done or what you've said? The overwhelming majority of women would likely answer without hesitation, "What I've said!" Our tongues get us into more hot water than we'd care to remember. How can you fix that problem?

The problems created by an untamed tongue are well-documented in the Bible. You don't have to read very far in the book of Proverbs—or Ecclesiastes, for that matter—before you're brought up short once again by an admonition to watch not only what you say but also how often you open your mouth to speak. In the Gospels, Jesus often spoke about the problems of the tongue, and the book of James devotes an extensive section to vivid descriptions of the uncontrolled tongue.

Why are there so many warnings about the words you speak? The reasons are plentiful, and many of them obvious: if you're not careful, your words can hurt others, be taken the wrong way,

> You will say the wrong thing if you talk too much—so be sensible and watch what you say.
> **Proverbs 10:19** CEV

> One of the basic causes for all the trouble in the world today is that people talk too much and think too little.
> **Margaret Chase Smith**

and bring dishonor to God, for starters. But there's a less obvious reason why God wants you to watch your tongue: your words reveal what's in your heart.

Blessed is the man who, having nothing to say, abstains from giving us worthy evidence of the fact.
—George Eliot (Mary Ann Evans)

Jesus expressed it this way: "A good person produces good things from the treasury of a good heart, and an evil person produces evil things from the treasury of an evil heart. What you say flows from what is in your heart" (Luke 6:45 NLT). God wants your words to reflect the goodness in your heart—but if your heart still holds traces of animosity, jealousy, and similar negative emotions, you're better off keeping your mouth shut until you've allowed God to deal with you in those areas. Otherwise, if you profess faith in God yet continue to slander, gossip, or in any way speak ill of others, you bring shame to God's name and to his other followers.

But how can you possibly watch every word you say? In the course of a single day, you may speak tens of thousands of words, depending on the nature of your lifestyle or your job. Stopping to think carefully about each sentence you utter just isn't feasible. Fortunately, there are only two simple rules you have to follow: keep what the Bible calls a "clean" heart, and talk a lot less. "Create in me a clean heart, O God," David prayed in Psalm 51:10 (NKJV). Clean and pure words flow from a clean and pure heart. And the fewer words you speak, the less likely you are to say the wrong thing at the wrong time. *The Message* paraphrase of the Bible—often a source of blunt, in-your-face truth—offers this warning: "Don't shoot off your mouth, or speak before you think. Don't be too quick to tell God what you think he wants to hear. God's in charge, not you—the less you speak, the better" (Ecclesiastes 5:2).

Look at Matthew 5:34–37, the passage known as the Sermon on the Mount. Jesus was advising the people never to make promises they couldn't keep. Jesus told them, "You only make things worse when you lay down a smoke screen of pious talk, saying, 'I'll pray for you,' and never doing it, or saying, 'God be with you,' and not meaning it. You don't make your words true by embellishing them with religious lace. In making your speech sound more religious, it becomes less true. Just say 'yes' and 'no'" (MSG).

Watch your words, but while you're doing so make sure you're also working on your heart. Keeping silent while you continue to harbor negative feelings is a foolproof prescription for a life of bitterness, resentment, and depression. Let your words be few, and when you do speak, let your words reflect a heart that's turned toward God.

The Bible describes the right words spoken at the right time as "apples of gold in settings of silver"

(Proverbs 25:11 NKJV). What a beautiful image! Wouldn't it be wonderful if your words could reflect that image? They can—any time you offer words of encouragement and hope to another human being.

what's essential

 Given the amount of trouble that the tongue can cause—and perhaps has already caused in your own life—a wise woman would heed everything the Bible has to say about it. Following the advice of biblical writers should keep you and your tongue out of hot water in the future.

DO think carefully before you speak, making sure that your words reflect well on God.

DO pay close attention to the condition of your heart and the words that flow from it as a result.

DON'T talk unnecessarily and thereby increase your chances of saying something inappropriate.

DON'T ignore the seriousness of the many biblical warnings about the harm that the tongue can cause.

Dare to Obey God

Be honest now—what comes to mind when you hear someone say that you have to obey God? Rigid adherence to rules? Strictly following a moral and ethical code? How about the words adventure, privilege, *and* joy? *No? Well, a life of faith can involve those three words, along with a journey like no other.*

Obedience doesn't exactly conjure up images of fun and excitement. And given the seriousness of choosing between a life with God and a life apart from him, the ultimate decision about whether to obey God shouldn't be taken lightly. But once you make that choice—once you decide that you will live for God no matter what—you can count on spending the rest of your life in a way that you never could have imagined, provided you do what God wants you to do.

That's really all obedience is, doing what God wants you to do. Yes, that means following the moral and ethical principles outlined in the Bible, but it also means following the specific guidance he gives you personally. That guidance can involve anything from a routine detour in your plans for

We truly love God only when we obey him as we should, and then we know that we belong to him. If we say we are his, we must follow the example of Christ.

1 John 2:5–6 CEV

When God gives a command or a vision of truth, it is never a question of what He will do, but what we will do. To be successful in God's work is to fall in line with His will and to do it His way. All that is pleasing to Him is a success.

Henrietta C. Mears

the day to a serious disruption in your long-range plans to a sacrifice of major proportions. Is it all fun and excitement? Obviously not. But following God's direction yields results that you can experience, like the peace that comes when you obey; and results you cannot see, like the impact of your obedience on people you'll never meet.

God is God. Because He is God, He is worthy of my trust and obedience. I will find rest nowhere but in His holy will, a will that is unspeakably beyond my largest notions of what He is up to.
—Elisabeth Elliot

Obedience to God is much more than following the rules.

Obeying God is an *adventure.* In her book *Forever Ruined for the Ordinary,* Joy Dawson wrote, "Have you ever said, 'If only I could hear God's voice, I would do whatever He told me'? Many years ago. That's exactly what I said . . . I took off on the adventure of a lifetime—hearing and obeying God's voice. I was forever ruined for the ordinary." Over the past forty years, the New Zealand missionary has preached and taught the Bible in fifty-five countries. Her life has proven to be anything but ordinary, all because she said "Yes" to God.

Obeying God is a *privilege.* The apostle John considered obeying God to be an act of faith and love, and he assured the early Christians that obedience would never be burdensome (1 John 5:1–4). Indeed, Jesus himself had said, "My yoke is easy and My burden is light" (Matthew 11:30 NKJV). Some have considered serving God to be such a privilege that they compare it to the story of Jacob, who loved Rachel so much that the seven years he labored to earn her hand in marriage seemed like just a few days (Genesis 29).

Obeying God is a *joy*. Jesus couldn't have stated it more clearly. Serving God brings joy to those who obey him: "If you obey my commands, you will remain in my love, just as I have obeyed my Father's commands and remain in his love. I have told you this so that my joy may be in you and that your joy may be complete" (John 15:10–11 NIV). In one of the many stories Jesus told his followers, he quoted a grateful master praising his faithful servant: "Well done, good and faithful servant; you were faithful over a few things, I will make you ruler over many things. Enter into the joy of your lord" (Matthew 25:21 NKJV). Jesus clearly referred to the joy God and his followers share in a relationship based on faithfulness.

Obeying God is a *journey*. Look at some of the journeys of obedience described in the Bible: Abraham's journey from Mesopotamia to Canaan, beginning in Genesis 12; the Israelites' journey from Egypt to the edge of the promised land, described in the book of Exodus; Paul and other missionaries' journeys in the book of Acts and the New Testament letters.

Adventure. Privilege. Joy. Journey. When you dare to obey God, that's what's in store for you.

interesting to note

In a theological context, obedience is considered an ongoing heart attitude, seldom referring to a single act of obeying God. Obedience refers to repeated and continuous acts of compliance with God's commandments, leading, and an intentional turning of your heart and mind toward God.

God, who got you started in this spiritual adventure, shares with us the life of his Son and our Master Jesus. He will never give up on you. Never forget that.

1 Corinthians 1:9 MSG

Your journey of obedience to God is in one sense like any trip you've taken. It's not one long, tedious journey; it's a trip made up of many small segments. If you remain obedient on each leg of the journey, when you stand before God you'll hear these precious words: "Well done, good and faithful servant!" (Matthew 25:21 NIV).

what's essential

The New Testament makes it clear that the extent to which you obey God is the best indication of how much you really love him. When you do what he asks you to do—which can sometimes involve a certain amount of risk—you affirm your faith in him as well as your love for him.

DO decide today that you will do whatever God asks you to do.

DO look forward to a lifetime of adventure, privilege, and joy as you embark on your journey of obedience to God.

DON'T consider God's commandments and precepts to be burdensome.

DON'T risk losing your peace by being disobedient to God.

Follow God's Lead

A number of passages in the Bible refer to the faith journey as a race. So it's a good thing to start running and stay in the running. But it's never a good thing to run ahead of God. When you let him take the lead and keep pace with his timing, you prove yourself to be a true follower of God.

Ⓐs you read Scripture, every now and then you come across a story that seems completely out of place, and you wonder why it was ever included in the Bible in the first place. Such is the case of the story of Tamar found in Genesis 38. Judah, a significant figure in biblical history, had chosen Tamar to marry Er, his oldest son. But Er died before he and Tamar had children, which under Israelite law meant that Tamar would be given in marriage to the next-eldest unmarried son—in this case, Onan.

But Onan wanted nothing to do with that arrangement, because any child he had with Tamar would be legally considered a child of Er and would inherit Er's estate, which Onan wanted for

God asks us to stop trying to work things out in our own way and depend on him and his timing . . . I am learning the truth of God's Word when he whispers, In the time of my favor I will answer you (Isaiah 49:8).

Marilyn Hontz

himself. He agreed to the marriage but took precautions to avoid getting Tamar pregnant. Soon enough, though, he died as well.

Twice widowed, Tamar was now expected to wait until Judah's youngest son, Shelah, was old enough to marry her. She did—but Judah reneged on his assurance that the marriage would take place. It's important at this point to try to understand the thinking of an ancient tribal culture in which marriage, childbearing, and lineage were of utmost importance. Tamar was expected to produce an heir for Er, her deceased first husband, through an arranged marriage with Er's closest living relative. It's also important to understand that Judah played a critical role in God's plan for the human race, and his lineage was a significant part of that plan.

When I am dealing with an all-powerful, all-knowing God, I, as a mere mortal, must offer my petitions not only with persistence, but also with patience. Someday I'll know why.
—Ruth Bell Graham

Here's where the story veers away from that plan. While we don't know how God intended to produce an heir in Judah's family, it certainly appears as if Tamar decided God needed a bit of human help. Knowing that Judah made a habit of having sex with prostitutes, Tamar disguised herself as one, enticed Judah to have sex with her, and became pregnant by him. As you can imagine, Judah was shocked to learn that he had slept with his daughter-in-law and that he would be the one producing Er's heir.

We don't know God's original plan for keeping Judah's lineage alive. But we can be fairly certain that having Tamar prostitute herself was not part of that plan. She ran ahead of God and cheapened herself in the process.

The story of Tamar is hardly uplifting. So why was it included in the Bible? Her story provides a record of Judah's lineage, which would have been important no matter what, but it was especially important for one main reason: Perez, one of the twins Tamar gave birth to, continued the bloodline that culminated in the birth of Jesus.

God turned this situation around, but both Judah and Tamar failed to keep pace with God's timing—Judah, because he refused to follow through with the marriage of Tamar and Shelah at the appointed time; and Tamar, because she became impatient and deceived Judah instead of waiting to see how God would work things out.

Waiting on God's timing is seldom easy, especially when you're waiting for one of his promises to be fulfilled. After all, he's God, and he can make things happen in an instant, so why can't he fulfill his promises in an instant? He can, of course—but it's critical that you follow God's lead, allowing him to bring things to pass in his own time and his own way, without any "help" from you. You may not always understand the reasons for his delay, but you can always trust him to make good on his promises at just the right time.

interesting to note

The Greeks had two words for time: *chronos* and *kairos*. *Chronos* refers to specific, measurable time, like 2:00 p.m. *Kairos* refers to concepts such as quality time or spending time with someone. Among people of faith, a *kairos* moment refers to a profound occasion in a person's life in which time seems to stand still.

At the time I have decided, my words will come true. You can trust what I say about the future. It may take a long time, but keep on waiting— it will happen!
Habakkuk 2:3 CEV

There will be times in your relationship with God when you'll become so excited about something he promised you that you'll want to make it happen right away. Remember that God knows you better than you know yourself, and he knows when you'll be ready to handle the fulfillment of that promise.

what's essential

 Learning to wait on God's timing—and having the patience to follow his lead rather than running ahead of him—is essential for those who are committed to seeing their faith journey through to the end. God seldom rushes things along. Getting used to his pace will help you in the long run.

DO learn to keep pace with God's timing by following him rather than running ahead of him.

DO trust God to fulfill his promises at just the right time, even if you can't understand his timing.

DON'T interfere with God's plan or timing by devising a scheme of your own to help him out.

DON'T be surprised to find gritty stories like Tamar's in the Bible; it's an honest book.

Love and Accept Yourself

Considering how much the Bible encourages you to focus on serving God and other people, it can come as a surprise to discover that it also tells you to love your neighbor as yourself. What's more, that concept presents a challenge to women of faith who daily strive to resist the culture of self-love that surrounds them.

How are you to make sense of what Jesus himself called one of the greatest commandments? And how are you to live it out? It's likely that, as a follower of God, the idea of loving yourself seems contradictory to your understanding of what God expects of you. In fact, your fundamental understanding of what it means to be a woman centers on the idea that you are to nurture others and care for their needs. You may also be among the many women who barely *like* themselves, let alone *love* themselves. You may live in a society permeated with me-first messages, but on a daily basis, you usually end up in last place on any list of priorities.

[Jesus said,] "You shall love the Lord your God with all your heart and with all your soul and with all your mind. This is the great and first commandment. And a second is like it: You shall love your neighbor as yourself."

Matthew 22:37–39 ESV

If you must love your neighbor as yourself, it is at least as fair to love yourself as your neighbor.

Nicolas de Chamfort

Before you get too hung up on the notion that Jesus is promoting self-love, take a look at what he said: "You shall love your neighbor as yourself." The wording of that statement implies that you already love yourself, and now you are to love your neighbor in the same way. Could it be that those first-century listeners understood his words far better than we do today? Among the many interpretations of his words is the one that suggests Jesus' remarkable teachings had so transformed their thinking—from oppressed minority to a people whom God loved wholeheartedly—that they had come to love themselves as a way of honoring God and showing their gratitude to him. Think about that. By loving yourself, you are so completely embracing God's love that you begin to actually believe you're someone worth loving.

 Believing you are loved will set you free to be who God created you to be . . . Rest in His love and just be yourself.
—Lisa Whelchel

That's a life-changing perspective, one that has the effect of shifting your focus off yourself and onto others. How? Throughout your life, you've accumulated a storehouse of memories of every embarrassing, sinful, unkind, and foolish thing you've ever done. That stockpile of memories has clouded your thinking about who you are. You see yourself as the sum total of all those mistakes, figure other people perceive you in the same way, and feel unlovable as a result. But guess what? God knows every single thing you've ever done—even the vast number of misdeeds you've long forgotten!—*and he loves you anyway*. When you really and truly grasp that truth, it will change your life. You can finally stop beating yourself up and worrying about what other people think of you. You're finally free to love your neighbor the same way you love yourself, as someone who is worth all the love God lavishes on you.

Loving and accepting yourself as God loves and accepts you brings you into full reconciliation with him. E. Stanley Jones, a twentieth-century missionary to India, described that reconciliation in this way: "You are no longer working against the grain of the universe; you're working with it . . . All self-hate, self-despising, self-rejection, drop away, and you accept yourself in God, respect yourself, and love yourself . . . You begin to move toward others in love. God moved toward you in gracious, outgoing love, and you move toward others in that same outgoing love."

Just think—the Creator of the universe "moved toward you in gracious, outgoing love," despite your imperfections, your weaknesses, your past. In fact, he did so *because* of all that. He wants to become the perfection in your life. He wants you to draw on his strength. And he wants you to walk with him into such a wonderful future that the uncomfortable memories from your past will begin to fade.

You will do all right, if you obey the most important law in the Scriptures. It is the law that commands us to love others as much as we love ourselves.

James 2:8 CEV

God loves and accepts you unconditionally. Return the favor by learning to also love and accept yourself, the person he created.

Reminding yourself of God's love for you as soon as you wake up can set the tone for the rest of your day. Make it a habit to fall asleep thinking about God's love, and ask him to remind you of his love for you first thing in the morning. Imagine how such a simple habit could change your perspective, both day and night!

what's essential

 The result of loving yourself is one of the many paradoxes of your life with God. Instead of turning your focus inward, self-acceptance liberates you to love others without any thought of yourself. Eliminating self-rejection allows you to get on with the life God wanted for you all along.

DO honor God by loving and accepting yourself—his creation.

DO love others in the same way that you now love yourself.

DON'T dwell on the memories of past failings.

DON'T confuse a godly acceptance of yourself with the kind of self-love inherent in a me-first mentality.

Let Your Life Shine

You? The light of the world? That's right. That's exactly what Jesus said. When you have the Spirit of God living inside you, you radiate his light, illuminating the dark places in people's lives that cause such sorrow and heartache. And most of the time, you never even realize how much hope your light has brought to others.

A s your relationship with God grows more intimate, you may begin to receive puzzling expressions of gratitude from the people in your life. You have no idea what they're talking about when they say things like, "Thank you so much. You cannot imagine how much you helped me!" All you remember are random encounters when you listened to a friend share her heart or offered a bit of encouragement to a stressed-out coworker or asked your cousin how you could pray about her situation. You scratch your head and wonder if they've got you confused with someone else.

They haven't confused you with anyone else, though someone else—the Holy Spirit—has

[Jesus said,] "You are the light of the world. A city that is set on a hill cannot be hidden. Nor do they light a lamp and put it under a basket, but on a lampstand, and it gives light to all who are in the house."

Matthew 5:14–15 NKJV

People are like stained-glass windows. They sparkle and shine when the sun is out, but when the darkness sets in their true beauty is revealed only if there is light from within.

Elisabeth Kübler-Ross

clearly played a role in all those interactions. When things like that start to happen, you can rest assured that the light of God is shining through your life. You say you don't see any evidence of God's light when you look in a mirror? That's a good thing. If you could see the way your life shines with the light of God, you could start to believe that you had something to do with all those encounters your acquaintances are so grateful for.

 As a countenance is made beautiful by the soul's shining through it, so the world is made beautiful by the shining through it of God. —Johann Georg Jacobi

The thing is, you can't turn on the light of God in your life, but you can certainly turn it off. How? By stifling God's activity in your life and allowing darkness—in the form of questionable thoughts and pursuits—to creep in. Think about that. If God were to allow his light to shine through you at a time when you're engaged in a pursuit that's contrary to his will, it would appear as though he had placed his seal of approval on what you were doing. No, you won't be able to illuminate the darkness in other people's lives and bring them hope while you're wallowing in the darkness yourself.

But back to the light. Numerous Bible verses underscore the significance of light in your life, as well as God's promises to use you to bring light to the world. Here are a few:

- "Because of God's tender mercy, the morning light from heaven is about to break upon us" (Luke 1:78 NLT).

- "If then your whole body is full of light, having no part dark, it will be wholly bright, as when a lamp with its rays gives you light" (Luke 11:36 ESV).

- "Everyone who lives by the truth will come to the light, because they want others to know that God is really the one doing what they do" (John 3:21 CEV).

- "You used to be like people living in the dark, but now you are people of the light because you belong to the Lord. So act like people of the light and make your light shine. Be good and honest and truthful" (Ephesians 5:8–9 CEV).

- "If we walk in the light, as he is in the light, we have fellowship with one another, and the blood of Jesus his Son cleanses us from all sin" (1 John 1:7 ESV).

Convinced? If you're still not quite sure that your life is all that radiant, remember that the light shining through you is not of your own making. You can't manufacture it, and you can't manipulate it. What you can do is bring God's light to your family, your neighborhood, your community, your workplace, and all your relationships by allowing God to light up your own life—your heart, mind, body, and soul. God's light is the hope of the world, and you can help bring that hope to the world by letting his light shine in your life.

The greater the transparency of a pane of glass, the more light is able to shine through it. Likewise, the more transparent you are—the more honest, open, and vulnerable you are with others—the brighter will be the light of God.

what's essential

 When you submit your life to God, the Holy Spirit becomes involved in every interaction you have with others. Whether you sense his presence is beside the point. He is there, transforming seemingly simple encounters into profound opportunities for God to shine through you to bring hope to the world.

DO be so submitted to God that you can't help but radiate the light of Jesus.

DO allow God to illuminate the dark corners of your own life so the two of you can deal with them together.

DON'T expect to recognize the light of God working in the lives of others through you.

DON'T put out God's light by engaging in activities that you know would displease and dishonor him.

Joy

You'll go out in joy, you'll be led
into a whole and complete life.
The mountains and hills
will lead the parade, burst-
ing with song. All the trees
of the forest will join the
procession, exuberant with
applause. No more thistles,
but giant sequoias, no more
thornbushes, but stately
pines—monuments to me,
to GOD, living and lasting
evidence of GOD."

Isaiah 55:12–13 MSG

Where Christ is, cheerfulness will keep
breaking in.

Dorothy Sayers

Happiness has to do with reason, and only
reason earns it. What I was given was the thing
you can't earn, and can't keep, and often don't
even recognize at the time. I mean joy.

Ursula Le Guin

Be a Woman of Integrity

Join the company of good men and women, keep your feet on the tried and true paths. It's the men who walk straight who will settle this land, the women with integrity who will last here.

Proverbs 2:20–21 MSG

Conventional wisdom can lead you to believe that the only way to get ahead, especially in business, is by cutting corners, turning a blind eye to questionable practices, or engaging in unethical activities—as long as you don't get caught. But God's wisdom is anything but conventional, and his wisdom says just the opposite.

The *Message* paraphrase of the Bible quotes God as saying, "I'll turn conventional wisdom on its head, I'll expose so-called experts as crackpots" (1 Corinthians 1:19). That's what he's done through the ages, turning upside down and inside out any "wisdom" that doesn't originate from him. Today, conventional wisdom has failed in so many segments of society that it's difficult to find one where it hasn't. And one aspect of that wisdom is ethics—an aspect that has failed monumentally.

Despite the fact that many universities require ethics courses in such fields as business, law, medicine, and journalism, ethical practices in those fields are exposed with nearly predictable

Integrity is not a given factor in everyone's life. It is a result of self-discipline, inner trust, and a decision to be relentlessly honest in all situations in our lives.

John Maxwell

182

regularity. Left in the wake of those practices are people who have suffered injury, loss, and even death. But even those who aren't directly affected also suffer loss—a loss of trust in corporations and institutions that once stood for integrity.

In the next verse of 1 Corinthians 1, Paul asked these questions: "Where can you find someone truly wise, truly educated, truly intelligent in this day and age? Hasn't God exposed it all as pretentious nonsense?" (v. 20 MSG). Yes, God has exposed the wisdom of the world as pretentious nonsense. But the answer to the first question may come as a surprise: you can find someone truly wise, truly educated, and truly intelligent in our day and age in business, law, medicine, and journalism—and every other walk of life. That's because God's people are everywhere, and those who place a high value on integrity are doing their part, in big and little ways, to restore the trust that has eroded over the years.

 The foundation stones for a balanced success are honesty, character, integrity, faith, love, and loyalty.
—Zig Ziglar

People of integrity may be just as ambitious and goal-oriented as anyone else, but commitment to always do the right thing outweighs every alternative. Fear of being caught doesn't even enter their minds; they do the right thing because it's the right thing to do, plain and simple. Those who are followers of God care little about any punishment a human being could inflict on them. Their concern, rather, is that everything they think, say, and do would be pleasing to God.

interesting to note

Tom, the Hebrew word for *integrity*, can be translated as "sound" or "complete." When you have integrity—and you either have it or you don't, as there's no such thing as partial integrity—you are of sound character and complete with regard to having what it takes to act morally and ethically.

I know, my God, that you examine our hearts and rejoice when you find integrity there.

1 Chronicles 29:17 NLT

The passage in 1 Corinthians continues to describe just how foolish that kind of integrity appears to people who reject the wisdom of God. Two writers known for their succinct sayings couched that sentiment in more contemporary language. Charles Caleb Colton, an English minister who lived at the turn of the nineteenth century, wrote this: "Nothing more completely baffles one who is full of tricks and duplicity than straightforward and simple integrity in another."

Baffle them or astonish them—either way, your integrity will impact some people in such a way that you'll have them wondering what's up with you. What a great opportunity to tell them that what's up with you is nothing short of your close relationship with God, a relationship that means so much to you that cutting corners, ignoring questionable practices, and engaging in unethical activities wouldn't even occur to you!

Integrity requires determination and discipline—the determination to resist the pressures and temptations that you face every day and the discipline to rely on the Holy Spirit to empower you to follow through. If you want to please God and become known as a woman of integrity, adopt that determination and discipline as your own—and trust in God's Spirit to give you the wisdom and power to do what's right.

Many people maintain their integrity in part by keeping a close watch on their thoughts, attitudes, and behaviors. One way to do that is to regularly examine how you handle challenging situations. One result will likely be your surprise at how many big and small ethical decisions you make in a single day.

what's essential

 Integrity is so important that losing it has costly consequences. Aside from losing the trust and respect of those around you, you also bring dishonor to God. Maintaining your integrity can also cost you—your job, your investments, your material possessions. But you'll never regret any loss that results from doing the right thing.

DO develop the determination and discipline it takes to be a woman of integrity.

DO count the costs of losing your integrity as well as maintaining it.

DON'T buy into the conventional wisdom that encourages dishonest practices to get ahead.

DON'T let the fear of getting caught be your motivation for doing the right thing.

Prepare Yourself for Good Things

Trained athletes know as well as anyone just how painful discipline can be. But they also know that the payoff for that discipline can far outweigh whatever agony they've had to endure. And that payoff can come in forms that offer as much satisfaction as an Olympic win or a major-league contract.

Jackie Joyner-Kersee is one of those athletes who can seemingly do it all. She's won five Olympic medals and holds the world and national records in several events, including the grueling seven-event heptathlon. One sports magazine named her "Female Athlete of the 20th Century," ESPN named her one of the "50 Greatest Athletes," and several sports commentators have called her the greatest athlete *ever*—of either gender.

Not bad for a woman who quietly suffered with asthma throughout her career.

Joyner-Kersee's discipline as a track-and-field athlete and Olympic competitor involved a great deal of sacrifice, pain, and suffering, and she was richly rewarded for that. But she turned all the

I've never been one who thought the Lord should make life easy; I've just asked Him to make me strong.

Eva Bowring

accolades and awards into a cause much bigger than her own benefit. The fame that resulted from her hard work gave her a platform from which she could share her deep faith in God and inspire others to lead a disciplined life immersed in God.

You don't have to be an athlete to understand the spiritual analogy in Joyner-Kersee's story, especially given that the life of faith is often compared to a race—a marathon, to be specific. Even if you've never run a marathon—or a half-marathon or any other competitive race, for that matter—you know this: you have to train in advance. You can't just get up one morning and decide to compete in a race of twenty-six–plus miles that same day—or that same week or month.

The surest test of discipline is its absence.
—Clara Barton

The analogy between a competitive race and a life of faith isn't a perfect one; few analogies are. Marathon runners need to start training long before their first race, while your faith journey begins the moment you place your trust in God. Faith more closely resembles on-the-job, or on-the-track, training. But remember, you're training for a marathon—an endurance race—and not for a sprint.

What does that mean in relation to the journey of faith? It means that you have to pace yourself by building up your spiritual muscle in increments, trusting God with your everyday life rather than putting everything on the line in one glorious act of faith before you even understand how God is working in

interesting to note

In 2 Timothy 2:5, the apostle Paul wrote this: "If anyone competes in athletics, he is not crowned unless he competes according to the rules" (NKJV). In Paul's day as now, that meant a runner had to stay within the lines of his lane— a likely reference to the "narrow gate" Jesus mentioned (Matthew 7:13 NKJV).

Prepare your minds for action; be self-controlled; set your hope fully on the grace to be given you when Jesus Christ is revealed.

1 Peter 1:13 NIV

your life. The religious landscape is littered with discouraged people who believed that God would perform some great miracle—like making them millionaires or bringing their loved ones back from the dead—before they took the time to get to know God and the way he operates. You don't want to be among them, even though your on-the-job training may seem to be longer and more painful than you ever imagined it would be.

One of the best ways you can make your spiritual training more effective is by trusting God more than you trust your own feelings. Think about Joyner-Kersee again. More than we will ever know, she experienced days when she had to believe she could compete even though she felt her lungs wouldn't cooperate. You'll have days when you need to keep believing that God is with you even though you don't feel his presence, that God loves you even though you don't feel his love, and that God hears your prayers even though you don't feel as if he's listening.

Prepare yourself for good things by submitting to God's discipline and training now regardless of how painful and unpleasant it may seem as you're going through it. Keep looking forward to that "peaceful fruit of righteousness" (Hebrews 12:11

ESV)—the "peaceful harvest of right living" (NLT)—that awaits you at the finish line.

You need stamina to run the race of faith. That requires several elements athletes need, in addition to regular exercise—which in your case is spiritual exercise. Those two elements are good nutrition (feasting on the Bible's nuggets of wisdom) and plenty of rest (relaxing in the knowledge that God is in control).

what's essential

 The journey of faith is a slow and steady exercise in trusting God; it's a race of spiritual endurance and not a competition to see who reaches the finish line first. Decide now that you will stay in the race, no matter how difficult it may get.

DO exercise your spiritual muscles to keep yourself toned and ready for any faith challenge.

DO look forward to the reward at the finish line.

DON'T look at the faith race as a sprint; you're in this for the rest of your life.

DON'T rely on your feelings, but trust in God and what he has said.

Be Honest with Yourself

Dishonesty in any form is wrong, but when you're dishonest with yourself, you make your life miserable, often without even realizing what the problem is. And that makes self-deception an especially difficult problem to deal with, because you're likely to be the last person to know you're deceiving yourself.

Because of the privilege and authority God has given me, I give each of you this warning: Don't think you are better than you really are. Be honest in your evaluation of yourselves, measuring yourselves by the faith God has given us.

Romans 12:3 NLT

Walking your talk is a great way to motivate yourself. No one likes to live a lie. Be honest with yourself, and you will find the motivation to do what you advise others to do.

Vince Poscente

Are you the "always late" type? You insist that *this* time you'll be on time for work—but you still arrive late. Once you get there, you try to convince your boss that the traffic was worse than usual, and it slowed you down so much that all the nearby parking spots were taken, making you even later than you would have been. And if it hadn't been for that slow elevator . . .

Whether that describes you or not, do you hear how, well, ridiculous all that sounds? Yet it's not uncommon to hear people make one excuse after another for their behavior—or to make those excuses yourself. What energy they expend trying to come up with a story that explains why they behave the way they do! If they were only honest with themselves, they could use their energy in a far more productive way by working to change the behavior they're trying so hard to excuse. And meanwhile, other people can readily see how dishonest they are with themselves, and as a consequence, with others.

 Our lives improve only when we take chances, and the first and most difficult risk we can take is to be honest with ourselves.
—Walter Anderson

That's no way to live. But how can you work to change behavior that you're blind to? Assuming, of course, that you really are blind to it; sometimes we know exactly what's wrong with us, but we don't want to admit it. Other times, though, we really are deceived. Here are some questions you can ask yourself to figure out how honest you are about your own nature and behavior:

Do I ever sound as if I'm making excuses for the things I do—or don't do? You couldn't get that report done for your boss because you had too many calls to return or the computer program you needed to use was acting up or you felt like you were coming down with something and didn't want to overdo it that day. Even though there may be a kernel of truth in all that, when you know deep down that you really didn't want to compile that report, the dishonesty embedded in those excuses is much bigger than that kernel.

Do I sound like I'm justifying my behavior? In addition to all the excuses you just gave, there's this: you shouldn't be responsible

Blessed is the man against whom the LORD counts no iniquity, and in whose spirit there is no deceit.

Psalm 32:2 ESV

for that report anyway. It's outside your job description, and even though you agreed to compile it as a favor, you're within your rights in putting it off—or not doing it at all. That's justification—coming up with seemingly logical reasons for why you should or shouldn't do something, even though those reasons run counter to what you know is the right thing to do—or not do. And that's dishonest.

Am I placing the blame elsewhere? Well, the *real* reason you didn't finish (or start!) the report is that accounting didn't get the information to you that you needed, and it's their responsibility to do that. Well, maybe—but you could have gone to the accounting department and gotten what you needed for yourself.

Do you see how much effort it takes to cover up whatever flaw prevented you—or the woman in this example—from getting the report done? If you tend to procrastinate, admit it and ask God to help you correct that. If you feel overwhelmed by a project, admit it and ask God to help you rein it in. If you don't understand something, admit it and ask God to help you understand it. And if you just don't want to do something, admit it and ask God to give you the desire to follow through with your commitment. Life is too short and too valuable to waste time deceiving yourself—especially when you have a relationship with the one who called himself truth itself (John 14:6).

When you hear yourself making excuses, justifying your behavior, or blaming others—even if you're hearing it only in your head—stop and ask God to reveal the nature of your self-deception to you. Ask him to bring light into those areas of your character that you're blind to and that need to be worked on.

what's essential

 Being honest with yourself not only helps you recognize the things you need to correct, it also helps you to have a better relationship with God and other people. Transparency is a likable quality in everyone, but you can't be transparent when you're trying to hide important aspects of who you are.

DO have the courage to see yourself as you truly are.

DO ask God to reveal flaws in your character that you are blind to.

DON'T try to hide your true nature from others; those closest to you can see it anyway.

DON'T make excuses, try to justify, or blame others for flaws in your own character.

Love Your Family

Don't be harsh or impatient with an older man. Talk to him as you would your own father, and to the younger men as your brothers. Reverently honor an older woman as you would your mother, and the younger women as sisters.

1 Timothy 5:1–2 MSG

Whether you're single or married, as long as you have living relatives, you have a family. And honoring that family with your love, care, and concern—defending them when necessary, protecting them when possible—brings God's favor on your life, even if your family can be accurately defined as dysfunctional.

It's the trend today to glibly describe every family as dysfunctional. But that's not accurate at all. Every family is flawed and imperfect, because every person is flawed and imperfect. But when it comes to the family, the definition of "dysfunctional" is specific, referring to unhealthy interaction. If you are in a truly dysfunctional family, the dynamic isn't simply imperfect; it's actually toxic, threatening the emotional and mental health of its individual members.

But even if your family—whatever shape that takes in your life—is genuinely dysfunctional, God not only wants you to honor your relatives, he also expects you to if you want to receive his blessing. Deuteronomy 5:16 says this: "Honor

Call it a clan, call it a network, call it a tribe, call it a family: Whatever you call it, whoever you are, you need one.

Jane Howard

your father and your mother, as the LORD your God has commanded you, so that you may live long and that it may go well with you in the land the LORD your God is giving you" (NIV). The New Testament calls this "the first commandment with a promise" (Ephesians 6:2 NLT).

What does it mean to "honor" your family? First and foremost, it means to love each member of your family. That includes any who have hurt you, but don't try to love those family members with anything other than the love God gives you. Your love won't be genuine or long-lasting, and you could end up more resentful than you may already be. Ask God to love those family members for you as he works on transforming your heart and your attitude toward them.

 The family unit plays a critical role in our society and in the training of the generation to come.
—Sandra Day O'Connor

Honoring your family also means forgiving them. Some relatives and some offenses are obviously much easier to forgive than others. You can probably forgive your son for wrecking the family car much more readily than you can forgive your cousin for coming on to your husband—or your husband for liking it. Forgiving your sister for ruining your favorite dress is nothing compared to forgiving your brother for sabotaging your efforts to get your dream job at the company where he works. You need the Holy Spirit's guidance and power to forgive those more difficult transgressions.

interesting to note

The biblical understanding of what constitutes a family is much broader than that in contemporary culture. The Hebrew word for family translates as "tribe," while the Greek word means "lineage." In biblical times, your family included everyone you descended from, which is why many genealogies were included in the Bible.

You honor your family also by spending time with them. Think of your own family and those things that distract you from being with them—or being with them fully. If you're part of a family living under the same roof, does anything come between you, such as overworking, friends, or the myriad forms of entertainment that lure you away? Your family is much more important than that, and you may not realize it until it's too late. If you're single and your family lives elsewhere, is anything keeping you from calling or visiting them? If so, what? Overcome whatever obstacles there may be—again, before it's too late.

Finally, you honor your family by taking care of them. This is a tough one for many women today, especially those who have a job, children at home, and elderly parents who need a caregiver. That's clearly a situation in need of divine direction! But taking care of your family also means simply providing for their needs—physical, emotional, and spiritual, to whatever extent you can do so. Whether you're taking your aunt to the doctor, listening to the latest drama in your niece's life, or praying over the phone with your sister a thousand miles away, you're honoring your family by taking care of them.

Maybe your family really *is* dysfunctional. No matter what, you know your family is flawed.

If you honor your father and mother, "things will go well for you, and you will have a long life on the earth."

Ephesians 6:3 NLT

Whatever the case, honor the members of your family. God placed you with your family; honor him by honoring them.

Sometimes the disputes that keep relatives apart are amazingly simple to resolve. If God shows you an opportunity to repair a rift in your family, take full advantage of it. You don't want to have regrets later on over missing a chance to bring the people in your family back together again.

what's essential

 God placed you in your birth or adoptive family for a reason. Likewise, if you are married, you are in that relationship for a reason, even if God was not a part of your decision to marry. You may not be able to *see* the reason, but you can trust God to assure you that there *is* a reason.

DO remember that God wants and expects you to honor your family.

DO forgive each member of your family, though you may need more time and an extra measure of grace to forgive some relatives.

DON'T buy into the lie that all families are dysfunctional; yours may just be flawed.

DON'T ignore any opportunity you may have to patch up differences among family members.

Be a Good Friend

Do a favor and
win a friend forever;
nothing can untie that
bond . . . Friends come
and friends go, but
a true friend sticks
by you like family.

Proverbs 18:19, 24 MSG

There's no question that most women excel at friendship and at relationships in general. That doesn't mean those friendships are perfect; in fact, when women allow themselves to be vulnerable with each other and let their imperfections show, that's when true friendship emerges.

Most women need deep friendships in their lives. They need at least one other woman with whom they can share their deepest thoughts and their wildest dreams. That level of intimacy requires trust, and trust is possible only in an atmosphere of honesty and vulnerability. But too often, women, particularly women who are trying to live a life pleasing to God, are afraid to admit that they're not perfect, and they find it hard to share their shortcomings, failings, and doubts with other women—especially if those women seem to have it all together. The reality, of course, is that there isn't a single woman on earth who has it all together. Realizing that makes it easier to be transparent with others.

Don't bypass the
potential for meaning-
ful friendships just
because of differences.
Explore them. Embrace
them. Love them.

Luci Swindoll

But there's another barrier to genuine intimacy among women, and that's the shame and humiliation women experience when the people they feel responsible for mess up their lives in a big way. So a woman whose son is arrested on a drug charge in a faraway city keeps that information to herself, holding in the pain and keeping up the appearance of having it all together. Do you know who gets hurt by that? She does, of course, but so does every other woman in her life who is hurting. Her pretense creates a barrier that prevents other women from coming clean about the pain in their own lives. And so the charade continues, with each woman holding in the pain and keeping up the appearance of having it all together.

 Everyone has a gift for something, even if it is the gift of being a good friend.
—Marian Anderson

What an unhealthy way to live! What's especially disturbing is that too often, when others find out what's really going on, they become judgmental rather than empathetic—all because of the pretense that was actually a mask for the pain. What a vicious cycle is created when people fail to share their hurts with each other.

Look at your own circle of female acquaintances—not close friends, but maybe coworkers or neighbors you don't know that well. Is there one among them who seems to live a charmed life—great house, handsome husband, well-behaved children, no visible problems? Maybe you've even felt envious of her, and that has subtly affected the way you treat her. But instead of assuming she has it all together, try this: assume there's some deep pain in her life that she is afraid to show the world. Wouldn't that change your attitude toward her? You might even try to befriend her if you really believed she was hurting.

You give the potential friends in your life a precious gift when you give them permission to remove their masks by sharing your own flawed life with them. It's not easy being the first one to drop the pretense, but it's essential to developing close relationships—and anyone who's been hiding her pain for the sake of appearances is in deep need of true friendship.

Throughout this process, let the Holy Spirit be your guide. If you reveal too much about yourself too soon—or you expect her to be more open than she's ready to be—you can sabotage the entire process before your friendship has a chance to take root.

Once it does, don't forget that flawed people can't help but have flawed relationships. You say the wrong thing, do the wrong thing, forget an important milestone, fail to acknowledge an accomplishment—the list of things one person can do to hurt a friend is seemingly endless. When you acknowledge those hurts, either as the perpetrator or the victim, you're being real and authentic.

If your friend can do the same, the two of you are well on your way toward a lifelong friendship.

Holding your pain inside you doesn't do you any good, nor does it help the other women in your life to share their pain with you. When you do bare your soul to someone else, be sure to also share your hope in God; don't leave your friend without hope for her own situation.

what's essential

 Solid friendships are built on a foundation of trust, and authenticity is essential to earning the trust of another person. Pretension has no place in an intimate friendship. Drop any pretenses in your own life, and encourage your friends, and potential friends, to do the same.

DO be transparent and vulnerable when it comes to your flaws and the problems in your life.

DO reach out to women who seem to be hiding their pain behind a mask of pretension.

DON'T be afraid to let others know that you don't have it all together either.

DON'T assume that the women you envy are leading lives any less flawed than your own.

Gifts

God has also given each of us different gifts to use. If we can prophesy, we should do it according to the amount of faith we have. If we can serve others, we should serve. If we can teach, we should teach. If we can encourage others, we should encourage them. If we can give, we should be generous. If we are leaders, we should do our best. If we are good to others, we should do it cheerfully.

Romans 12:6–8 CEV

When I stand before God at the end of my life, I would hope that I would not have a single bit of talent left and could say, "I used everything you gave me."

Erma Bombeck

No one can arrive from being talented alone. God gives talent; work transforms talent into genius.

Anna Pavlova

Be a Peacemaker

There's a story in the Bible about a tense situation in which a foolish man offended the future king, provoking his wrath and intention to exact revenge. But this incredibly foolish man had an equally incredible wife, and her peace-making skills not only saved the day for her and all Nabal's household, but they also earned her a place in the palace.

You're blessed when you can show people how to cooperate instead of compete or fight. That's when you discover who you really are, and your place in God's family.

Matthew 5:9 MSG

Abigail, the heroine of this story, was married to a wealthy rancher named Nabal. The fact that Nabal's very name meant "fool" gives a clue to the kind of nature he had. Abigail probably had her hands full throughout their marriage cleaning up after the foolish mistakes he made. That on-the-job training served her well when David and his men, who were hiding from King Saul, camped out near Nabal's property. After helping Nabal's shepherds protect their sheep, David sent several of his servants to ask Nabal for some food.

Although they were considered by some to be fugitives, David and his contingent of about six hundred men had behaved honorably toward

We are not at peace with others because we are not at peace with ourselves, and we are not at peace with ourselves because we are not at peace with God.

Thomas Merton

Nabal's workers. The men greeted Nabal in peace, even referring to themselves as his servants (1 Samuel 25:8). But Nabal refused their request for food, insulted David to them, and set them on their way. David did not take kindly to this response. When Nabal's shepherds got wind of what Nabal had done and what David planned to do—which wasn't pretty—they immediately notified Abigail and sought her help.

You can never have an impact on society if you have not changed yourself . . . Great peacemakers are all people of integrity, of honesty, but humility.
—Nelson Mandela

Abigail hadn't even done anything yet, and we already know a great deal about her. The herdsmen went to her for help. In an ancient tribal culture where the man of the household was the undisputed boss, it speaks volumes about Abigail's nature that the shepherds trusted her not only with the information but also with the situation itself. "Know this and consider what you should do, for harm is determined against our master and against all his house, and he is such a worthless man that one cannot speak to him," one servant told Abigail (1 Samuel 25:17 ESV).

Abigail's strategy in attempting to smooth things over was brilliant. She set about to prepare and provide an abundance of food for David and his men. When she approached David with her gift, she humbled herself before him, acknowledged that Nabal's treatment of him had been wrong, assumed responsibility for Nabal's actions even though she had been unaware of the encounter until the herdsmen spoke with her, and praised

David's positive character traits—in particular, those that contradicted any desire for vengeance.

She further pointed out the consequences David's revenge would have in the future. Killing Nabal would be nothing short of murder, and when David became king, which was inevitable, such an action would come back to haunt him as he attempted to unify the country. Nabal may not have been highly respected, but he was wealthy and powerful within his own tribe, and killing him would be political suicide.

David immediately recognized the wisdom in Abigail's approach: "Blessed be GOD, the God of Israel. He sent you to meet me! And blessed be your good sense! Bless you for keeping me from murder and taking charge of looking out for me . . . Return home in peace. I've heard what you've said and I'll do what you've asked" (1 Samuel 25: 32–33, 35 MSG).

Nabal didn't realize it then—he was back at home, drinking the night away—but he had escaped certain death thanks to his wife's negotiating and peacemaking skills. Ten days later he was not so fortunate; after hearing the whole story, he suffered a stroke, fell into a coma, and eventually died. Apparently, Abigail made quite an impression on David during their brief encounter,

interesting to note

In contrast to her husband's name, *Abigail* means "fountain of joy." For reasons unknown, since the turn of the millennium, Abigail has consistently placed in the top ten popular names for baby girls— quite a jump after placing between 94th and 176th as recently as the 1980s.

Do not repay anyone evil for evil. Be careful to do what is right in the eyes of everybody. If it is possible, as far as it depends on you, live at peace with everyone.
Romans 12:17–18 NIV

because as soon as he heard about Nabal's death, David proposed marriage to her. She accepted, married David, and later became the queen of Israel.

Abigail's strategy could form the curriculum for a master class in negotiation. Her success is all the more remarkable given the status of women at the time; the urgency of the situation demanded that she ignore her society's conventions and use the talents God had given her—despite her gender.

what's essential

 Humility, vulnerability, and acquiescence are important qualities when it comes to peacemaking—along with courage and a tough skin. Without a healthy dose of each of these traits, you could do serious damage to a situation that might otherwise be peacefully resolved.

DO strive to restore and keep the peace whenever you're involved in a conflict.

DO learn peacemaking skills from Abigail's story in 1 Samuel 25.

DON'T make matters worse by attempting to excuse inappropriate, offensive, or insulting behavior.

DON'T underestimate the importance of making amends and urging cooperation; the consequences could be life-changing.

Master Money

With all the finance-related books on the market, Web sites on the Internet, shows on radio and television, and seminars in cities big and small, you have many sources to turn to when you decide it's time to get your finances in order. Just don't ignore the most important source: the Bible.

On the surface, it may appear that going to the Bible for financial advice is like going to an accountant for spiritual counseling. But the Bible has a great deal to say about money and the right way to handle it, and the best part is that the advice doesn't come from the latest popular financial guru but from the eternal source of wisdom in every area of life, God himself.

The foundation for all the biblical advice about handling money can be summed up in the verse above found in Matthew 6:24. That verse forces you to make a fundamental decision: will you serve God, or will you serve money? You can't have it both ways, because serving money—running after wealth and more wealth—will

No one can serve two masters. For you will hate one and love the other; you will be devoted to one and despise the other. You cannot serve both God and money.

Matthew 6:24 NLT

My God will meet all your needs according to his glorious riches in Christ Jesus.

Philippians 4:19 NIV

distract you from what should be your primary purpose in life, serving God.

There are other ways of "serving" money than just accumulating riches. The very word *serving* implies that money is your master, even if you have little money. If you've been living beyond your means or making unwise decisions about your money, you're likely in deep debt. No matter how passionate you may be about the work you do, when you're in debt you're working to serve money, a master who shouldn't have had anything to do with your passion in the first place.

 Never work just for money or for power. They won't save your soul or help you sleep at night.
—Marian Wright Edelman

Even if you're somewhere in between—neither chasing after the big bucks nor steeped in consumer debt—you're serving money if you are envious of those who have it or the myriad things money can buy.

But how can you stop serving money—stop being so focused on making it, having, it, spending it, investing it—and begin serving God instead? The biblical answer is actually quite simple. You could avoid spending lots of time and money on learning about the latest and greatest formula for financial success by following the timeless formula found in just a few verses in the Bible. First of all, give your undivided devotion to God and trust him to provide for your needs (Matthew 6:33; Philippians 4:19). Second, give, give again, and keep on giving (Luke 6:38 and many other verses).

Other Bible verses make reference to money, particularly in the book of Proverbs, where you'll find a crash course in financial management based on wisdom and common sense. In a nutshell: don't be greedy or lazy; don't borrow or hoard money; don't trust in wealth or the prospect of making easy money. Instead, trust God, work hard, earn your money the honest way, and give to others.

That's much less complicated than any financial plan devised by humans, and it's much easier to remember. Plus, it doesn't have a mere six-month track record for success. Wise people have been following God's advice for millennia, and that advice is just as sound today as it was when he first communicated it to his people. And thankfully, God's plan isn't affected by market fluctuations or real-estate appraisals or the value of the dollar against the yen.

Some people place the total number of money-related verses in the Bible at twenty-three hundred, indicating that this is a pretty important topic to God. He knows how easily people can turn away from him in pursuit of wealth, and he knows how easily people can turn against one another for the same reason. Don't let a focus on money come between you and God or create problems between you and those you love. It's not worth it. Jesus underscored that assertion when he asked the

interesting to note

Acts 5:1–11 tells the tragic story of two early followers of Christ, Ananias and Sapphira. Their greed and love of money prompted them to first withhold the truth and then to tell an outright lie. As a consequence, they both lost their lives.

It is easy to be independent when you've got money. But to be independent when you haven't got a thing—that's the Lord's test.

Mahalia Jackson

people of his day, "What good would it do to get everything you want and lose you, the real you? What could you ever trade your soul for?" (Mark 8:36–37 MSG).

All the biblical wisdom specifically related to money management can be summed up in the advice to live within your means. That applies even to giving; you can't give more than you have without incurring debt. And debt is an even harsher master than money itself is.

what's essential

 Giving is one of the most important principles of God's system of money management. You'd find it a challenge to meet someone who has joyfully given to others and now regrets it. People who give generously discover that their giving has resulted in a newfound lightness and freedom in their lives.

DO decide that you will serve God rather than the pursuit of wealth.

DO pray about your finances and follow God's wisdom for managing your money.

DON'T let money come between you and God or create conflict with others.

DON'T follow the advice of the latest financial guru unless it lines up with Scripture.

Do Justice and Love Mercy

To many contemporary observers, justice and mercy have strict definitions from God's perspective. They perceive justice as meting out punishment, no matter how harsh. They perceive mercy as letting the guilty get away with murder, at least metaphorically. But justice and mercy have other definitions.

In contemporary society, the word *justice* has become so closely linked with criminal justice that people often overlook the ways in which justice exists in the routines of everyday life. The word *mercy* is similarly misunderstood; it isn't simply the pardon one receives from the criminal justice system, which is the polar opposite of justice. In fact, in our everyday lives, justice and mercy are two sides of the same coin; you can practice both at the same time.

Look at the verse above in Micah 6. It asks an important question: just what *does* God require of you after all? Other Bible verses give different answers, but none of them contradict Micah 6:8. Doing justice and loving kindness (another word

He has told you, O man, what is good; and what does the LORD require of you but to do justice, and to love kindness, and to walk humbly with your God?

Micah 6:8 ESV

If we could just figure out how to have more fun at it, maybe more of us would join the ranks of those who seek after justice and mercy.

Robert Fulghum

for mercy) in a spirit of humility is to become integrated with all the other things God requires of you. Micah 6:8 refers to our attitude toward other people, not the institutional principles of the criminal justice system.

 Being all fashioned of the self-same dust, let us be merciful as well as just.
—Henry Wadsworth Longfellow

Here's how the three requirements look with regard to followers of God in the twenty-first century:

Do justice. In the context of the Bible, the justice referred to applies to God's wisdom and judgment in relation to the downtrodden of society. We are to "do justice" to the oppressed and marginalized, those who have neither the voice nor the money to see that they are treated fairly. When you do justice in this sense, you become the advocate of the weaker members of society, the poor, the hungry, the needy. In the Bible, that advocacy extended to widows, orphans, the fatherless, and strangers to the tribe or community. In our culture, those segments may or may not be oppressed. The contemporary interpretation is to find the powerless and empower them by allowing God's power to work through you.

Love kindness. Mercy is kindness and compassion along with a host of other qualities, like benevolence, that may or may not apply to specific situations. One story in the Bible (found in Luke 10:25–37) tells of a man who was robbed, beaten, and left on the side of the road to die. Because of certain cultural taboos associated with this man's heredity, several people of different social strata and tribes ignored him. But one man, known ever since as the good Samaritan, not only offered physical assistance but also paid for his care. That's mercy—kindness and compassion toward someone society expects you to shun.

You can show mercy in so many ways: forgiving a debt when you know the person who owes you is going through a hard time; deciding not to sue someone whom you have every legal right to sue; reaching out and actually touching an outcast, such as a filthy, smelly homeless woman.

Walk humbly with your God. Among God's requirements is that you walk with him and acknowledge him as your God. That's critical to doing justice and loving kindness, because in order to meet those requirements, you need to do so in the context of your relationship with God.

Then there's the "humbly" aspect. If you are to be effective in doing justice and loving kindness, you need a spirit of humility. You need to humble yourself before God and those you are to serve. The downtrodden don't need the help of someone who comes across as superior to them; they need someone whose compassion is so genuine that she can put herself in their position, no matter how foreign their situation is to her.

interesting to note

Hebrew scholars consider the word *mishpat*, the word for *justice* used in this verse, to be the fundamental principle of Hebrew law. It refers to a transparent judicial system in which all the facts and the truth of a matter are disclosed and decisions are rendered in a just, fair, and upright manner.

By the help of your God, return; observe mercy and justice, and wait on your God continually.
Hosea 12:6 NKJV

Do justice. Love mercy. Walk humbly with your God. That's what God requires of you.

Find out which organizations and ministries to the oppressed operate in your area, and find out all you can about the best ways you can help out. Make sure that you bring God into the process; he'll guide you toward a way of helping that will make the best use of the gifts and talents he's given you.

what's essential

 Learn to apply the heart attitude inherent in Micah 6:8 to all the other ways you serve God and other people. If you use justice, mercy, and humility as the guiding principles in all your interactions with others, you're guaranteed to please God, help meet the needs of others, and bring hope to their lives.

DO be aware of opportunities for practicing justice and mercy in your everyday life.

DO empower the powerless by allowing God's power to work through you to bring justice to their lives.

DON'T add to the burden of people in distress by demanding what you believe they owe you.

DON'T approach the needy and oppressed with an attitude that conveys superiority.

Serve Others

One of the hallmarks of an authentic life with God is the desire to serve others. But too many people fail to serve others because they don't know what they're equipped to do, they aren't aware of the myriad volunteer opportunities available to them, or they think they don't have enough time.

Awoman named Dorcas was a widow who lived in the town of Joppa. It's not known how long she had been widowed, but the book of Acts indicates that she was an important part of the community of Christians in the city. Acts 9:36 says this about her: "She was always doing kind things for others and helping the poor" (NLT). Few Bible verses describe people solely in terms of their service to others, but Dorcas, also known as Tabitha, is an exception. She had what is commonly called a servant's spirit, a nature that gravitated toward helping other people.

When Dorcas became ill and died, several of the local Christians went to a nearby town to beg Peter to come. The sense of urgency in their message seems to indicate that they believed if Peter

Those of us who are strong and able in the faith need to step in and lend a hand to those who falter, and not just do what is most convenient for us. Strength is for service, not status. Each one of us needs to look after the good of the people around us, asking ourselves, "How can I help?"

Romans 15:1–2 MSG

When we step out in faith and offer all we have, God will use it in powerful ways. How much is enough? Just what we have when God is with us!

Jane Douglas White

prayed for her, Dorcas would come back to life, even though her body had already been prepared for burial.

Peter arrived to discover a scene that spoke volumes about Dorcas and her life: "The room was filled with widows who were weeping and showing him the coats and other clothes Dorcas had made for them" (Acts 9:39 NLT). Imagine that sight: Peter rushing to Joppa in response to this urgent request, Dorcas's lifeless body awaiting burial—and a group of widows sobbing and holding up garments Dorcas had made for them to make sure Peter saw them. What a tribute to Dorcas! The women clearly loved her and wanted to make sure others knew what she had done for them.

Faith is the first factor in a life devoted to service. Without it, nothing is possible. With it, nothing is impossible.
—Mary McLeod Bethune

The scene was such a sight that Peter had to ask everyone to leave the room so he could pray over the body. He began praying and commanded Dorcas to get up—and she did. She not only opened her eyes, but she also sat up with Peter's help. It's no surprise that the news spread quickly, and many people in that area came to faith in Christ as a result.

Dorcas simply did good deeds, helped the poor, and sewed garments for the widows. She wasn't a renowned preacher; she wasn't highly educated or even highly skilled. But she did what she could, and her community loved her for it—so much so that they sent for Peter. And Dorcas was raised back to life as a result.

That's really all that service is: doing what you can for others with a pure heart, with no thought of recompense or reward.

Many women naturally gravitate toward serving others; it's part of the nurturing aspect of a woman's character. But they often limit themselves to traditional ways of serving that may not represent their strengths—like trying to provide homemade entrées for potluck dinners when their real strength lies in buying a fresh veggie platter at the supermarket.

The opportunities for service in your community are limited only by its population. Ask God to give you a desire to serve and guide you toward an area of service appropriate for you. Be open to any and every possibility. Are you all thumbs? Habitat for Humanity uses volunteers who fit that description and perform functions like holding a ladder or running errands for the crew. Is compassion your strength? A nonprofit hospice often needs nonmedical volunteers to give full-time caregivers a break, simply sitting with a patient who may not even be aware of their presence. But the caregiver, often a spouse or other relative, is aware—and grateful for an hour or so away from the house.

You don't need special skills or a lot of spare time to serve others. All you need is willingness—and the always reliable leading and power of the Holy Spirit.

interesting to note

One of the Hebrew verbs for "to serve" is the word *abad*, which can simply be translated as "to work" or "to labor." But it carries with it the connotation of working for someone else—and by further implication, to work as a subject of God.

My friends, you were chosen to be free. So don't use your freedom as an excuse to do anything you want. Use it as an opportunity to serve each other with love.

Galatians 5:13 CEV

217

Do you love animals? Volunteer with an animal shelter. Is hospitality your strength? Host a Bible study in your home. Do you have a reliable car? Offer to drive homebound patients to medical appointments. Your community needs your help. Even if you think you have little to offer, you can do more than you think.

what's essential

 A servant's heart can develop over time. Once you begin to serve other people, you may discover that this is part of your purpose in life—giving of your time and talents to make a difference in other people's lives.

DO look around your community—and your neighborhood—for opportunities to serve.

DO rely on God to show you an area of need where he can use you to help other people.

DON'T limit yourself to areas of service you're familiar with; expand your thinking to include unfamiliar terrain.

DON'T avoid serving others because you think you have to have lots of spare time to volunteer.

Prioritize the Essentials

You've heard the advice for years: you have to get your priorities straight! Who can argue with that? Of course you have to prioritize! But if you think that means creating a one-two-three-and-so-forth ranking of all the important things in your life, you'll be delighted to know that there's a simpler way to prioritize.

Seek first his kingdom and his righteousness, and all these things will be given to you as well.

Matthew 6:33 NIV

Seriously, now—have you ever tried to create a rank-order list of all the priorities in your life? As a woman, you know how challenging that is. Yes, of course, God tops the list. But then what comes next? Your second-tier priorities shift up and down the list throughout the day. You'd love to put Bible reading somewhere toward the top of your priorities, but the reality is that if you're a mother, for example, many other things will likely take priority over Bible reading. That doesn't mean you won't be able to carve out some time each day for the Bible; it just means that a rank-order list doesn't serve your purposes all that well.

We realize our dilemma goes deeper than shortage of time; it is basically a problem of priorities. We confess, we have left undone those things that ought to have done; and we have done those things which we ought not to have done.

Charles E. Hummel

See if this works better for you: scrap the priority list, which is an artificial structure to begin with, and visualize God encompassing everything in your life. Every moment of every day is saturated with the presence of God. Instead of worrying about whether God holds the top spot on your priority list, you can rest in the knowledge that he is in everything you do throughout the day. He's a part of every errand you run, every task you perform at work, every onion you chop, every load of laundry you do. See how much easier that is? Instead of "making time for God," you've consciously brought him into every big and little aspect of your day, and as a consequence you've spent the entire day with him.

 It is the mark of great people to treat trifles as trifles and important matters as important.
—Doris Lessing

If you still feel the need to prioritize, simplify the process by thinking in broad categories. What would come after God? Hopefully, the people in your life would be the next priority, but trying to rank those people in order of importance is probably counterproductive. If God is your all in all, if he's a part of everything you do throughout your day, he'll let you know whom you should focus on at any given moment. Doesn't this seem easier as well? No more deciding if your husband or children should come first if you're a married mother. Liberate yourself from that way of thinking by letting God guide you throughout the day.

People who try to organize their lives by a rank-order listing will tell you that the next item should be work (if it's your boss who's advising you) or church (if it's a pastor who's advising you). You may not even have a church—or a job for that matter. And what about the other lives you're responsible for, like your pets? They rarely make it onto any prioritizing lists, but if you've accepted responsibility for domesticated animals, you know what a priority it can be to just keep them alive and healthy.

Are you convinced yet that a priority list may not be the best way to arrange your life? What if Jesus himself offered you a method for setting your priorities in a way that's guaranteed not to fail? You're already familiar with this verse, but here it is in another version: "More than anything else, put God's work first and do what he wants. Then the other things will be yours as well" (Matthew 6:33 CEV). Your everyday human concerns include the need to determine what's most important at any given moment, and as long as your life is steeped in God, you can count on him to meet that need.

If prioritizing your life according to a ranking structure is more frustrating than effective, learn

interesting to note

In another verse about priorities, the apostle Paul said that love is more important than faith. That verse (1 Corinthians 13:13) has become so familiar, it's hard to imagine how startling that may have sounded to people who had lived in a rigid religious climate for so long.

Now abide faith, hope, love, these three; but the greatest of these is love.

1 Corinthians 13:13

NKJV

to see God permeating everything you do. As you remain connected with him, your priorities will fall into place, because he'll be leading and guiding you every step of the way.

Bringing God into every aspect of your life requires focus and attention. When you're at work or running errands or peeling an onion or starting the rinse cycle, take a moment to acknowledge God's presence and reestablish a conscious connection with him.

what's essential

 Seeking God is the most important thing you can do on any given day—and at any given moment. Not only does God honor you for turning to him, but you also benefit by virtue of the fact that your focus on God will affect your attitude and temperament throughout the day.

DO steep your life in "God-reality," relying on him to let you know what's important.

DO remain connected with God throughout the day, allowing him to lead and guide you.

DON'T become frustrated by a prioritizing method that doesn't work for you.

DON'T forget to think in terms of broad categories rather than minute details.